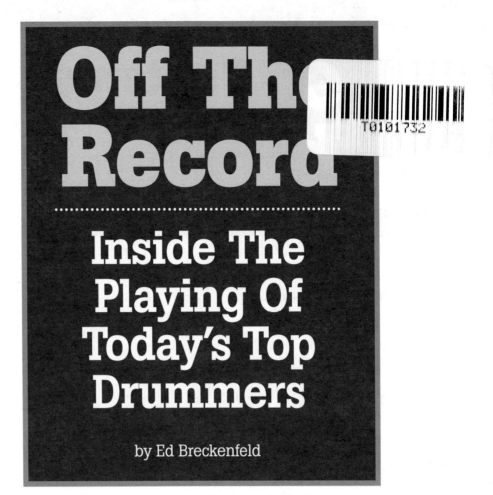

Off The Record

Inside The Playing Of Today's Top Drummers

by Ed Breckenfeld

Cover/Back Cover Photos Credits:
John Dolmayan, Dave Lombardo, Chad Smith, Travis Barker, and Adrian Young by Alex Solca
Taylor Hawkins, Questlove by Paul La Raia
Neil Peart by Andrew McNaughtan
Dave Grohl by Lissa Wales
Jimmy Chamberlin by Gene Ambo
Steve Gadd by Ebet Roberts
Bernard Purdie by Phillip Halyard
Matt Sorum by Ross Halfin
Alan Evans by W. Churgin

All sound files were created using FXpansion BFD 1.5 software.

Published By:
Modern Drummer Publications, Inc.
12 Old Bridge Road
Cedar Grove, NJ 07009 U.S.A.

Contents

Foreword

This book contains the best articles from *Modern Drummer* magazine's monthly *Off The Record* column. *OTR* takes a close look at the drumming on popular recordings through detailed transcriptions and analysis of the most interesting beats and fills. I began writing the column in June of 2001, and at first our focus was on new players and bands in a mostly modern rock vein. Over the years, through suggestions from readers, *Off The Record* has evolved to include classic performances from all styles of popular music.

In this volume we've collected the top drummers in each genre, including a few previously unpublished entries. We'll start by examining some of the best players in today's rock scene, move through rock's punk and metal offshoots, explore the worlds of funk and prog drumming, and then return full circle to look at some of the most influential rock drummers of the past.

Reading and working through this book is almost like having a drum lesson with each of these famous players. As a learning aid, we've included a disc of sound files demonstrating many of the most challenging patterns in the book.

The Art Of
Transcribing

Many readers have asked how I'm able to figure out the drumming on these recordings. Transcribing drum music involves several abilities, all of which can be developed. Any drummer who can read music can transcribe. The most important necessity is a thorough knowledge of drum techniques. Learn all that you can about your instrument. Listen closely to every recorded drum performance, even innocuous music on the radio and television. When you begin to recognize the drum patterns in much of what you hear, you're ready to begin transcribing.

You'll need to develop your ears. The ability to hear drum parts through the haze of guitars, bass, keyboards, and vocals is a must. Any recording experience you have will be helpful. In the studio you're able to hear instruments stacked one upon the other as you're building or mixing a song. Listening to a drum track by itself and then adding bass, guitars, etc. can help you to isolate and identify those sounds in other recordings.

You also have to be able to accurately identify the parts of the drumkit being played. When you're transcribing a drummer, put yourself in his shoes. He or she has four limbs just like you—what is each of those limbs doing? Start with the cymbal part. Do you hear a steady rhythm on the hi-hat? Or is it on the ride cymbal? What about the snare drum pattern? Is it just a backbeat, or are there some ghost notes in there? Are there crash cymbals or toms included in the beat? If so, one of the hands has to be picking those up. Now, what's the bass drum doing? Is it a single bass drum pattern or an obvious double bass? Finally, is there a left-foot hi-hat pattern that you can hear? Imagining yourself behind the drummer's kit, playing these parts, can help you identify which sound you're hearing.

Sometimes a recording isn't as clear as you'd like, or there's too much going on in the mix to hear it all plainly. There are a few things that can help you in these instances. First of all, being able to EQ (adjust the sound frequencies of) a mix is essential. I've picked out many a tricky hi-hat or cymbal pattern by cranking up the treble end of the EQ. Likewise, turning up the bass frequencies can help with bass drum parts. Sometimes I'll dial up the sub woofer on my computer speakers and rest my hands on the desk to feel the vibrations from the kick drum.

EQ helps in another way: If you turn down the midrange frequencies in most rock recordings you'll diminish the guitars and vocals and wind up with a clearer picture of the drum patterns. The fader settings on my EQ look like a big letter "U"—up on the bass and treble ends while sloping down in the middle. Drums pop out of the mix with this type of setting.

It's nice to be able to hear what you're transcribing on different sound systems. Sometimes listening on another pair of speakers can make something more clear. The most important piece of gear is a good set of accurate headphones. Quality headphones provide a superior separation of sounds than cheaper models. For example, many recording engineers place toms at different positions in a stereo mix. You can easily hear where a drummer switches from one tom to another in a fill as the sounds move around in the headphones. I do my most critical listening on headphones while using the EQ described above.

For the times when you're trying to transcribe something that is just too fast to grasp, slow-down software is helpful. The latest version of Windows Media Player includes a slow-down feature. Because it can make things sound a little disorienting, I wouldn't use it to transcribe whole songs. But when you need to find out if there are six or eight notes in that blazing double kick burst, slow-down software can make it easier to hear.

These are some of the techniques we put to use in creating *Off The Record*. Discovering exactly what your favorite drummers are playing can be a fascinating and insightful practice—a great way to learn new techniques and approaches. I hope this book will inspire you to try some transcribing of your own.

Ed Breckenfeld

Chapter 1

Modern Rockers

These are the drummers you hear on the radio, taking popular rock drumming into a new era with a combination of taste and technique. Each of these players has injected his personality into the music of his band. Some are veterans of earlier hit-makers, like Soundgarden's Matt Cameron, who's now playing with Pearl Jam, or Guns N' Roses' Matt Sorum, who was most recently scoring hits with Velvet Revolver. Others, like Linkin Park's Rob Bourdon and Wolfmother's Myles Heskett, are hot young players making a name in their breakthrough bands.

Longtime Smashing Pumpkins drummer Jimmy Chamberlin and Foo Fighters' Taylor Hawkins have enjoyed large followings in the drumming community for years, while players like Trapt's Aaron Montgomery and Army Of Anyone's Ray Luzier (now with Korn) are winning over new fans with their impressive chops. Scott Underwood of Train and Switchfoot's Chad Butler show that groove is still king in popular music. The future of modern rock drumming is in good hands with this generation of players.

Switchfoot's Chad Butler
The Beautiful Letdown

The fourth album from Switchfoot reached a wide mainstream audience with a positive message that stood in stark contrast to the darker sounds on modern rock radio. On *The Beautiful Letdown*, the band explores the region between hard-edged alt/rock and lighter pop, giving drummer Chad Butler a chance to showcase his versatility. Chad guides his band through driving rock grooves, heavy tom patterns, hip-hop beats, and the flow of 12/8 time with a steady hand. Let's check out a few of his groove ideas.

"Meant To Live"

Butler takes a page from Dave Grohl on his opening beat for the intro of the album's lead track and first hit single. (0:06)

The song's verses have a great sense of movement due to this floor tom groove, featuring some nice use of the small tom, along with snare flams and open hi-hat accents. (1:31)

TRACK 1

"Ammunition"

Chad creates his own drum loops on the kit rather than using a drum machine, like this syncopated pattern from the intro of the track. (0:01)

TRACK 2

In the song's verse, the drum part bounces back and forth from a slow-moving tom groove to a double-time rock beat. (0:50)

TRACK 3

"Dare You To Move"

Look for the subtle changes between the first and second measure in this two-bar verse pattern. Chad creates interest by simply swapping around a few bass and snare notes while maintaining the rhythm. (1:38)

"Gone"

The ever-so-slight swing in this beat sets a funky tone for the intro and verse of the song. (0:16)

The groove shifts into high gear when Butler switches to a hip-hop feel for the pre-chorus. (0:42)

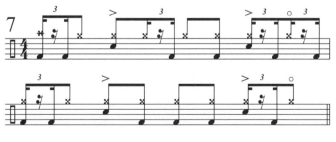

"Twenty-Four"

The album's closing track is a 12/8 ballad, with this re-entrance pattern near the song's ending. It highlights Chad's natural feel for this time signature. (3:31)

Army Of Anyone's
Ray Luzier

MUSIC KEY

open H.H.	O	R.C.	C.C.
T.T.			
S.D.			
F.T.			
B.D.1			
H.H. w/ foot		B.D.2	Add I T.T.

Propelled by the breakout success of the single "Goodbye," Army Of Anyone's self-titled debut won over modern rock fans with its blend of radio-friendly hooks and head-bobbing grooves. Though the band boasted a lineup of alt-rock royalty with former members of Stone Temple Pilots and Filter, AOA's secret weapon was ex–David Lee Roth drummer Ray Luzier. His performance on the album was up front and center, combining strong grooves with eye-opening fills that will have you reaching for the repeat button. Here are a few prime moments to check out.

"It Doesn't Seem To Matter"

The album opens with a tension-building 16th-note crescendo that culminates in a classic flam and bass drum fill before releasing into the powerful verse groove. (0:00)

Near the ending of the track, Luzier gives a taste of things to come with this 32nd-note flourish. The switch from six-note to four-note groupings gives the fill a palpable feeling of acceleration. (3:07)

"Goodbye"

Here's the blockbuster drum feature from the end of this hit single. Ray runs the gamut of double bass licks, with each idea receiving its own distinct presentation. This is a stellar display of technique, serving notice that Luzier is a force to be reckoned with. (3:13)

TRACK 4

"Non Stop"

The combination of a pair of single strokes with a three-note double bass ruff produces a flashy quintuplet, which Ray uses to kick this song off with a bang. (0:00)

Here's another great lick from later in the track. The accent pattern in this fill matches the guitar rhythms. By designing his ideas around the other bandmembers' parts, Luzier ensures that his chops-heavy fills are seldom out of context or gratuitous. (1:08)

"Disappear"

Ray's verse beat for this tune has the flowing feel of a 12/8 groove, even though the time signature is 4/4. This unique feel works well with the strummed rhythms of the guitars in the track. (0:05)

"Father Figure"

This song revolves around another cool groove. This time the toms drive the track's crunchy guitar riff. (0:05)

TRACK 5

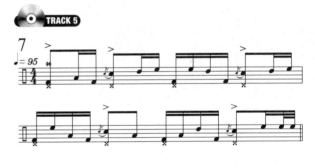

"Leave It"

Towards the end of this heavy song, Luzier squeezes plenty of excitement out of a fill that involves no kick drums. The syncopation in the second beat of the fill sets up the straight 32nd-note finish. (3:27)

Wolfmother's
Myles Heskett

The smash debut from Australian power trio Wolfmother is an homage to early-'70s British rock. Combine Robert Plant–style vocal imagery with Deep Purple–tinged guitar and organ riffs, wrap it in a vintage Frank Frazetta album cover, and you've got a young band that wears its influences like a badge of honor. For his part, drummer Myles Heskett brings the thunder from down under, bashing through these tracks with the straightforward approach of a bygone era. Here's a smattering of his best drum patterns from the album.

"Dimension"

The disc opens with Heskett's quarter-note snare/floor tom groove that deftly bolsters the song's guitar riff without adding clutter. (0:03)

"White Unicorn"

Myles' drum part for the instrumental bridge of this tune is right out of the John Bonham school of sweeping 16th note–triplet fills. The individual triplets in the first and third measures could be played with various stickings: RLRL (right-hand lead into a left-hand crash), LRLR (left-hand lead into a right-hand crash), or RLLR (which allows the right hand to start the rhythm and hit the crash). (2:42)

"Woman"

The middle section of this hit single features a couple of triplet riffs played by the whole band. Heskett uses his snare and toms to match the downward melodic movement of the first riff, followed by crash and snare combinations to support the second part. (1:24)

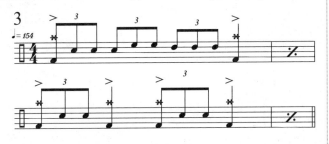

"Apple Tree"

Wolfmother has a knack for coming up with interesting instrumental passages. This speedy track shifts to a halftime feel, where Myles creates a pattern that switches between triplets and a heavy syncopated groove. (1:02)

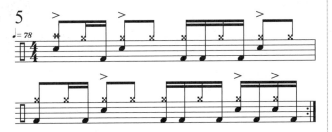

"Colossal"

In Heskett's two-measure beat for the verse of this plodding track, the two snare hits on the last beat of the second measure act like a fill, pumping a little energy into the end of the pattern. (0:23)

For the chorus, Myles expands on the syncopation of his verse groove and then uses a 16th-note crescendo to bring the band back to the intro riff. Notice the return of the two-note snare pattern in measure 3. This snare part becomes one of the motifs in the song. (1:00)

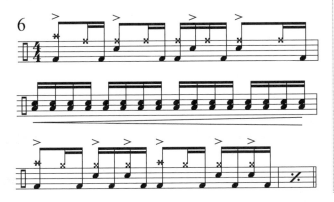

"Mind's Eye"

The slow, moody feel of this tune gives way to an organ-led double-time shuffle, with Heskett's well-placed bell accents providing rhythmic interest. (3:39)

"Witchcraft"

Myles shows off his versatility as the band takes a departure into 6/8 on this track. This syncopated groove is slightly swung, adding a jazzy element to the album. (0:07)

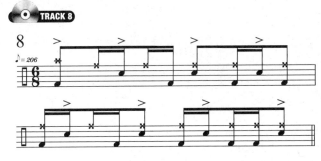

"Love Train"

Next, Wolfmother tries their hand at a mid-tempo '70s funk groove. Heskett hits all the right marks with his offbeat snare and kicks, ghost notes, and open hi-hat accents. (0:10)

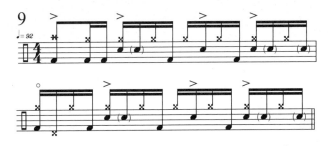

During the chorus, Myles' 16th note–triplet fills add to the retro flavor of the song. (0:42)

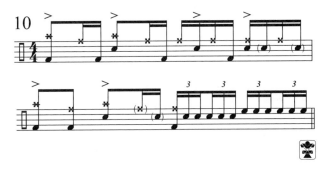

Pearl Jam's
Matt Cameron

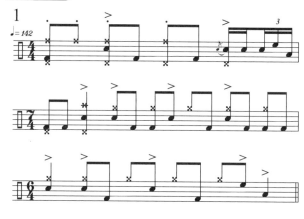

Pearl Jam's powerful and politically charged self-titled album was a return to form for the quintet from Seattle. Part of the credit goes to Matt Cameron, the ex-Soundgarden slammer who was on his third studio release as Pearl Jam's drummer. Matt's muscular yet tasteful grooves energize the band, driving them to rock harder than they have in a decade. And occasional odd-time sections certainly bear the Cameron stamp.

"Life Wasted"

The album's opening track displays Matt's well-known skill for making odd time signatures seem downright normal. In the song's pre-chorus, a potentially disorienting thirteen-beat sequence (divided into 7/4 and 6/4) is smoothed over by the flow of this syncopated groove. (0:31)

TRACK 9

"Comatose"

This two-minute speed burner features a cool Cameron beat during the bridge, with a twisting rhythm that propels the section's 16th-note guitar part. Matt's kick drum keeps things moving under an interesting sticking pattern. (1:23)

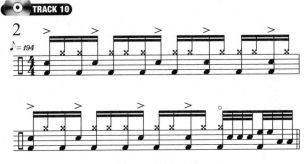

"Severed Hand"

Here's a good example of how a judicious use of kick and hi-hat can elevate a normal drum fill into something special. Try playing Matt's fill (measure 2) without his kick and hi-hat notes, and then add them in to feel how much of an impact they make. (1:48)

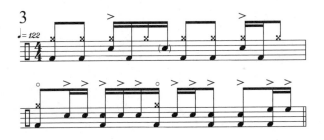

Near the end of the track, Cameron employs extra snare notes, loose hi-hats, and cymbal crashes to intensify the groove under the song's climactic lead guitar solo. (3:49)

"Marker In The Sand"

One of Cameron's greatest strengths is his ability to temper his percussive energy with sensitivity towards the band's lyrical message. The ebb and flow of this song's beat works well with Eddie Vedder's vocal phrasing in the chorus. (1:37)

"Unemployable"

Matt throws in some slick bell work during the intro of this tune. The 16th-note figure at the end of the second measure stands out because nothing else is happening in that brief spot. (0:07)

"Big Wave"

This song's fade-out section has Cameron's influence written all over it. As the groove switches from 4/4 to 5/4, Matt drops in offbeat crashes, open hi-hat accents, and explosive fills at will. (2:38)

"Gone"

In the second verse of this track, Cameron combines a couple of familiar hi-hat and rimclick patterns to create a compelling beat. (1:52)

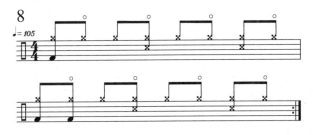

"Army Reserve"

There are two smooth grooves in this song. The first one is a relaxed semi-funk beat for the verse. (0:09)

The second groove occurs during the rolling 12/8 chorus. Matt changes from hi-hat to ride cymbal and uses a busier pattern to punch up the intensity of this section. (0:55)

Velvet Revolver's
Matt Sorum
Contraband

Ross Halfin

Supergroup Velvet Revolver was up and running with their much anticipated album, *Contraband*. Combining the best attributes of each member's previous band (Guns N' Roses and Stone Temple Pilots), Velvet Revolver produced a slew of radio-friendly rock hits. Throughout this disc, Matt Sorum delivers a performance that's as slammin' as ever. Let's check out a few of his drum parts.

"Illegal I Song"

Here's a great "in your face" intro from this rocking track. (0:00)

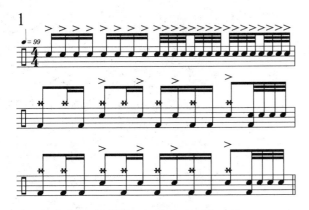

The song's chorus builds on the drum beat from the verse, releasing into a driving 16th-note-triplet fill. (0:46)

TRACK 12

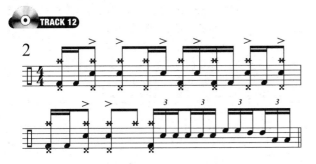

"Fall To Pieces"

Matt's entrance on the pre-chorus of this hit single is a textbook example of how to energize a power ballad. (0:42)

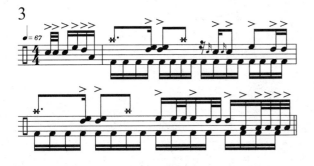

"Headspace"

The playful rhythmic shifts in Sorum's fills add interest throughout the album. (0:08)

"Superhuman"

Here's a classic kick/snare lick that works perfectly as a setup for an off-beat crash. (3:50)

"You Got No Right"

Matt blends his bass drum nicely into this fill near the end of the track. (4:42)

"Slither"

The album's first single opens with this menacing 16th-note tom groove. The four snare hits at the end of the measure act as a counterpoint to the heaviness of the toms and kick drum. (0:00)

TRACK 13

"Dirty Little Thing"

Here's another great fill that relies as much on the bass drum as it does on the snare and toms. (3:31)

TRACK 14

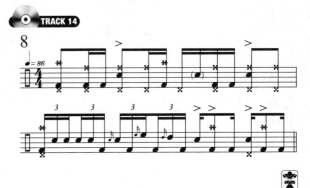

Foo Fighters'
Taylor Hawkins

One By One

Foo Fighters are blessed with having not one, but *two* of rock's best drummers. Dave Grohl, of course, also happens to be the band's lead singer, guitarist, and songwriter. On FF's *One By One*, however, he left the drumming in the capable hands of Taylor Hawkins, who responded with some of his finest recorded work. Here's a look at a few of Taylor's drumming highlights from the album.

"All My Life"

The album's high-intensity first single is sparked by offbeat snare/crashes that punctuate the intro guitar riff and a quick 16th-note fill setting up the verse.

TRACK 15

"Low"

Taylor's tom groove matches this track's backbone guitar riffs.

TRACK 16

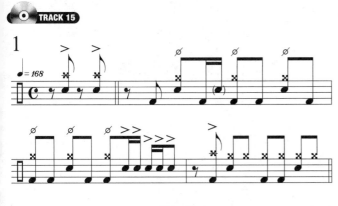

At the end of the song's instrumental section, the drums lay out for a bit, and then Taylor busts out with this blazing 16th-note-triplet fill.

"Times Like These"

This song features an intro in 7/4 time, which I've divided into 4/4 and 3/4 for clarity. Taylor flashes his Stewart Copeland influence with a short fill that finishes in an offbeat snare/crash at the end of this sequence.

"Disenchanted Lullaby"

The moody intro and verse of this tune are enhanced by the syncopated kick and snare placement in this pattern.

"Halo"

"Halo" contains some great drum fills, this one coming just before the first pre-chorus. Notice the bass drum 8th notes, which add to the excitement of the fill.

Taylor's groove for the song's chorus breaks away from his steady backbeat in the verse, as he locks in with the rhythm of Nate Mendel's bass line.

"Come Back"

The marching feel of the last chorus in this album closer lends weight to Dave Grohl's repeated vow, "I will come back!"

TRACK 17

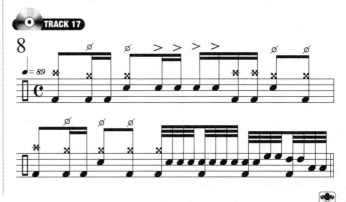

THE SMASHING PUMPKINS *GREATEST HITS*

Gene Ambo

I n this chapter we're going to take a look at one of the most important drummers to come out of the alt-rock movement. Jimmy Chamberlin had the perfect blend of technique and song sense to embellish Billy Corgan's tough/bitter-sweet sound. Jimmy could thrash it out one moment and display the finesse of a jazz drummer the next. The Smashing Pumpkins' *Greatest Hits* showcases some of his best work.

"Siva"

From the start, Jimmy whipped up the band's intensity with his fiery fills. This one comes out of a breakdown section.

"Rhinocerous"

Here's a dose of chops, with a jazz/fusion influence.

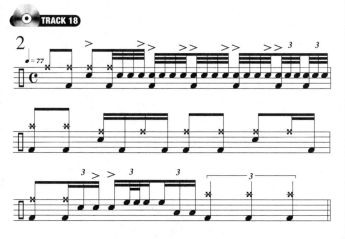

"Cherub Rock"

This well-known sequence from the song's intro is pure Jimmy Chamberlin.

"Today"

In the second measure of this verse pattern, notice the ghosted snare drag, followed immediately by an offbeat open hi-hat accent that punctuates the lyric "…greatest day I've ever known."

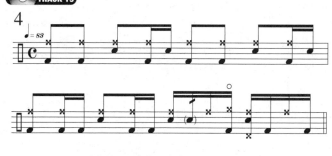

"Bullet With Butterfly Wings"

The chorus of this tune shows how Jimmy often plays off vocals *and* guitar accents at the same time.

"Tonight, Tonight"

In an intro heavy with strings, Jimmy takes an orchestral approach.

"The Everlasting Gaze"

After being out of the Pumpkins for a while, Jimmy returned as strong as ever. Here's a great snare drum lick from this song's choruses.

By the end of the tune, the groove is absolutely *cranking.*

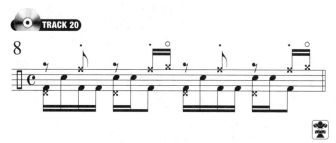

Train's
Scott Underwood
Drops Of Jupiter

Train drummer Scott Underwood lays down a solid pulse for the band's tunes, combining subtle dynamics with skillful technique. Here are some examples from the band's hit album, *Drops Of Jupiter*

"She's On Fire"

The album's opening cut immediately establishes Scott's relaxed funky groove, with *extremely* soft ghost notes and a great setup for the chorus.

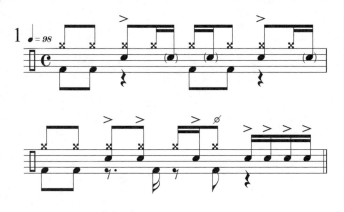

The bridge features crash cymbals and an open five-stroke roll.

"I Wish You Would"

Here's another syncopated beat, again with ghost notes adding depth to the feel.

TRACK 21

"Drops Of Jupiter"

The first hit single off the album has a slow hip-hop feel. Scott *swings* it to provide a deep pocket, with ghost notes once again playing a major part.

TRACK 22

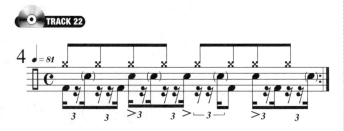

"Let It Roll"

This song opens with a rambling snare drum groove, spiced up with tom hits and open rolls.

TRACK 23

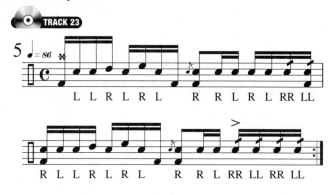

After a straight verse beat, Scott creates a unique ride cymbal/snare pattern for the chorus that recalls the feel of the intro. This is a very sophisticated bit of drumming!

TRACK 24

"Something More"

Here's a well-designed opening fill that sets the tone for this track.

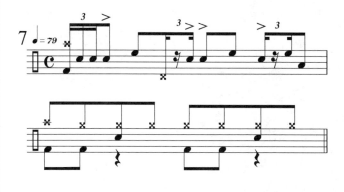

"Get Away"

Scott adds a jazzy feel to this 12/8 tune with more of his signature ghost notes.

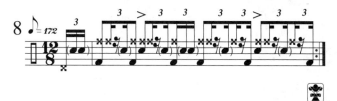

Linkin Park's
Rob Bourdon
Hybrid Theory

Linkin Park's platinum-selling debut album for Warner Bros. Records, *Hybrid Theory*, was a modern rap/alternative hybrid. As MC Mike Shinoda traded with vocalist Chester Bennington, drummer Rob Bourdon played off, around, and over machine patterns. Bourdon's solid drumming "brought the rock" to the band's musical mix.

"Papercut"

The album's opener begins with a few bars of a drum loop. Then Rob crashes in with his own version of the pattern.

"One Step Closer"

Linkin Park's first single features this groove and quick fill.

TRACK 25

During the climactic "shut up when I'm talking to you!" segment, Rob bashes louder on his hi-hats, while slightly varying the beat and fills.

TRACK 26

"With You"

Here's another syncopated pattern, this time with an offbeat snare thrown in.

"Crawling"

Rob's main drum part for this hit tune is a four-bar sequence with an unusual and compelling snare placement.

"Runaway"

The intensity builds steadily in this song, starting with a tight hi-hat verse groove.

Rob pounds out a jarring tom rhythm under the "gonna run away!" vocal chant.

TRACK 27

Finally, the message is driven home at the song's end by a quarter-

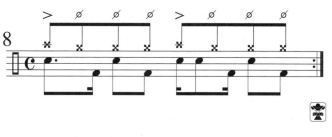

Trapt's
Aaron Montgomery

MUSIC KEY

Open	○	R.C.	C.C.
H.H.	✕		
T.T.			
S.D.			
T.T.			
B.D.			
H.H. w/foot		B.D.2	Add'l Toms

On their debut album, nü-metal band Trapt took the organic approach, preferring the time-tested combination of guitars, bass, and drums instead of loops and samples. And the band's tough, melodic sound won them widespread radio play. Good drumming is always crucial to this genre, and Aaron Montgomery delivered, laying down grooves with enough firepower to keep things exciting. Let's take a look.

"Headstrong"
This hit single contains a two-part chorus linked together by the following sequence, which features some of Aaron's slick bass drum work.

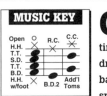

"Made Of Glass"
The middle of this song's bridge is highlighted by this explosive 32nd-note fill, which ends in a sweep around the drumkit.

"Hollowman"
Aaron's clever beat for the bridge of this track uses three-against-two polyrhythms to give the groove a near quarter-note-triplet feel.

"Still Frame"
This intro pattern is played on low toms and bass drum for a maximum powerful effect.

With all the syncopation in this drumbeat from the song's verse, the quarter-note accents on the hi-hat provide the driving momentum to keep the groove moving forward.

"The Game"
Aaron handles fast 12/8 time with assurance and ease. Check out this groove and wonderful fill from the end of this tune's instrumental section.

The climax near the end of the song features this rousing fill sequence.

"New Beginning"
Double bass provides the heavy groove in this 12/8 pattern based on the guitar riff from this song's intro.

Chapter 2

Heroes Of Punk

Like the music they play, the drummers in this category bring energy and an in-your-face attitude to their playing. The household names in this chapter are Dave Grohl and Travis Barker, whose influential drumming has left a giant mark on the genre. From over on the pop side of punk we have Weezer's Patrick Wilson, No Doubt's Adrian Young, and Zach Lind from Jimmy Eat World, while the garage rockers are represented by The Strokes' Fab Moretti and The Killers' Ronnie Vannucci. And for mainstream punk fans we include the dynamic Adam Carson from AFI and Steve Jocz from Sum 41. All are major hitters in the world of punk.

Weezer's
Patrick Wilson

The Green Album

Karl Koch

In 2001, the king nerds of punk/pop returned with their first album in five years. *Weezer* (called "the green album" by fans) contains ten two- to three-minute pop tunes that recall the big hits of the band's first CD. Gone was the loose, raw approach to the drum tracks used on Weezer's previous release *Pinkerton*. Instead, Patrick Wilson's drumming here was as direct, economical, and energetic as the songs themselves.

"Don't Let Go"

Here's a cool little chorus setup coming out of the song's guitar solo.

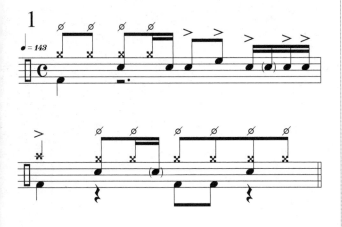

"Photograph"

Patrick uses a classic surf-style beat on this one, updated by riding on the crash cymbal.

"Hash Pipe"

The first single contains some of the best drumming on the album, including this Bonham-esque sequence from the pre-choruses.

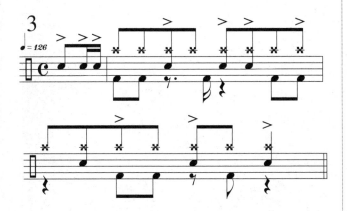

Patrick then switches to a dance groove on the ride cymbal for the chorus.

TRACK 31

"Crab"

This song features several hi-hat/bass drum breakdowns, creating tension and then releasing into long drum fills.

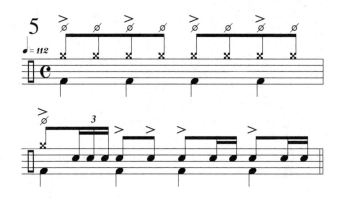

"Simple Pages"

Even short fills are infused with Patrick's personal style.

TRACK 32

"Glorious Day"

Another great short fill. Check out the bass drum note at the end of the measure. It serves as a pick-up to the next measure.

Jimmy Eat World's
Zach Lind

JIMMY EAT WORLD

Jay Blakesberg

Jimmy Eat World is a modern success story. Dropped by their first major label, the Arizona quartet's revenge was their self-titled CD featuring the smash hit "The Middle." The album's pop hooks infused with alt/punk energy have proved to be a radio-friendly combination. Zach Lind played with power and taste, laying the perfect bed for his band's pulsing 8th-note guitars.

"Bleed American"

The opening track sets the rocking tone for the album, as Zach matches his rhythms to Jim Adkins and Tom Linton's power chords.

"A Praise Chorus"

Zach's speedy, two-fisted tom groove slams home the bridge of this song. (The tom accents on the first and third beats are played as open flams.)

"The Middle"

In the breakthrough single, Zach sets up the chorus with a short tom fill, then locks his beat to the vocal melody.

"Your House"

Here's a great, unusual pattern from the bridge of this tune, adding an almost-Latin feel to Jimmy Eat World's pop sound.

TRACK 33

"Sweetness"

This hard-charging groove features catchy double snare hits on the fourth beat of each measure. Zach repeats this theme in the fill that leads into the choruses.

"Get It Faster"

Once again, Zach's drumming punctuates a guitar riff virtually note-for-note. This example is from the song's bridge.

"Cautioners"

This syncopated drum pattern adds a mechanical undercurrent to this slow, dreamy ballad.

TRACK 34

"The Authority Song"

Zach rides his floor tom for a '60s garage band feel in this intro beat. The one well-placed small tom note is a cool touch.

MUSIC KEY

Open	O	R.C.	X
H.H.	X		
T.T.			
S.D.			
F.T.			
B.D.			

After years as an indie band, AFI's first major-label release was a polished and radio-ready disc that brought this California punk quartet to the masses. But *Sing The Sorrow* was no sellout, as the band's writing and arrangements were more complex than ever, while their power and intensity remained intact. Carson showed a wide array of abilities on grooves ranging from hardcore to alt-funk, metal, and 12/8. Here are a few examples.

"The Leaving Song Pt. II"

This impressive tom pattern leads into a dark breakdown section in the middle of the track. Check out how Adam uses his bass drum to set up the snare/crashes.

TRACK 35

"Dancing Through Sunday"

Adam's compelling fill jumping out of the breakdown in this speed burner launches the band into a fiery guitar solo section.

"Girl's Not Grey"

The effectiveness of this double-time verse groove in the album's first single comes from unfilled space in the second measure, embellished by subtle semi-open hi-hats on the second and fourth beat.

The song's bridge features this smooth little marching-style snare drum sequence.

"The Great Disappointment"

This track weaves its way through a series of interesting groove changes. As the lengthy intro ends, Adam uses this pattern to set up the verse.

TRACK 36

When the song shifts to 12/8 in the chorus, Carson slips smoothly into this syncopated groove. The switch from hi-hat to ride cymbal further reinforces the change.

TRACK 37

"This Celluloid Dream"

Here's another effective verse setup. The first two bars of this sequence are from the end of the song's intro, and the short fill that ends on the second beat of the third measure works perfectly because the vocal begins immediately after the fill.

"...But Home Is Nowhere"

Adam slams home the start of each chorus in this tune with this powerful beat.

The Strokes'
Fab Moretti
Is This It

MUSIC KEY

Open	O	R.C.	
H.H.	X	X	
T.T.			
S.D.			
F.T.			
B.D.			

Drummer Fab Moretti's minimalist approach is a perfect match for the moody melodic sound of The Strokes. Eschewing fills and complicated beats for a simple, driving approach, Fab creates repetitive, trance-like grooves that are a major part of The Strokes' appeal. Let's check out a few of the grooves from *Is This It*.

"The Modern Age"

Fab cruises along on his snare and floor tom for the intro and verse of this song, then releases into the ride cymbal in the chorus.

"Soma"

One of the album's rare drum fills kicks this tune into its second chorus.

As the song moves to a close, Fab turns up the intensity with this beat.

"Someday"

This single opens with a classic double-time R&B drum figure. Fab builds the dynamics by adding hi-hat quarter notes to the pattern when the strumming rhythm guitar part comes in.

The chorus features open hi-hat hits on the downbeat to counterbalance the offbeats in the kick drum pattern. This creates a wonderful polyrhythmic effect.

"Alone, Together"

The guitar solo in this track begins over a pounding floor tom beat. When the solo becomes more syncopated, Fab follows by switching to the ride cymbal and adding offbeats on the snare.

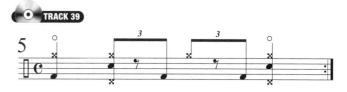

"When It Started"

Changing pace, Fab pulls out a funky little bass drum groove for this tune.

"Trying Your Luck"

Here's a couple of beats that effectively help contrast this song's sparse verse and busy chorus. The atypical snare placement in the chorus is what really makes the difference.

Box Car Racer's
Travis Barker

MUSIC KEY

	Open		R.C.	C.C.
H.H.	O		X	X
T.T.				
S.D.			(O)	
F.T.				
B.D.				
H.H. w/foot	X	Ghost Note		

Box Car Racer was a side project for one of the brightest lights of the early 21st-century drumming world: Blink-182's Travis Barker. Forgoing Blink's juvenile humor for a more sober vision, BCR allowed ample room for Travis to explore the creative art of the drumbeat. Mixed in with his unusual grooves was an obvious love for drum corps-style snare technique. It was an impressive combination.

"I Feel So"

The intro beat for the album's lead track imparts a revolving, circular feel to the song.

TRACK 40

Travis's chorus pattern locks rhythmically to the vocal line, "I Feel…So…Mad…. I Feel…So…Angry." Not even a *hint* of traditional snare drum here!

"Watch The World"

This beat is simply indescribable. Travis seems to be painting rhythmic impressions of the song's lyrics.

TRACK 41

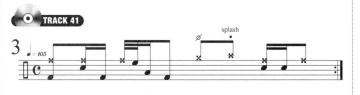

"Tiny Voices"

Here's another quirky, compelling groove, with Travis riding 16th notes on a rim while dropping in offbeats on the bass and snare.

TRACK 42

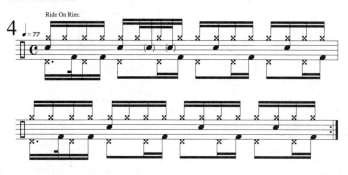

"Cat Like Thief"

This song opens with a beat that sounds like a conversation between the kick/snare pattern and the hi-hat. The alternating effect is completely cool.

"And I"

Here's a little of that Barker snare technique, sprinkled with some well-placed tom and hi-hat accents to make yet another outstanding groove.

TRACK 43

"There Is"

This smooth little drum corps figure sits nicely under the acoustic guitars in the track.

Sum 41's
Stevo 32
All Killer No Filler

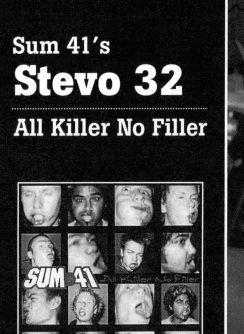

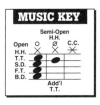

MUSIC KEY

	Semi-Open H.H.		
	Open	Ø	C.C.
H.H.	O	X	✳
T.T.			
S.D.	●		
F.T.	●		
B.D.	●		
	Add'l T.T.		

A few short years after forming in high school, Sum 41 went platinum with their first full-length album, *All Killer No Filler*. Although they may have been raised on Iron Maiden and Judas Priest, this Canadian quartet was pure twenty-first-century punk/pop. Drummer Stevo 32 (a.k.a. Steve Jocz) was a worthy successor to speed demons like Tré Cool and Chad Sexton. Check the tempo on some of these licks.

"Nothing On My Back"
Early in this tune, a half-time tom groove sets the mood.

TRACK 44

In the bridge, Steve returns to the toms for a syncopated solo break.

TRACK 45

"Never Wake Up"
Break out the hardcore!

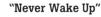

TRACK 46

"Fat Lip"
This driving funk pattern supports the guitar hook from the album's first single.

When the song shifts to double time, Steve kicks in the afterburners.

"Handle This"
Here's a great intro fill using flams and bass drum.

"Heart Attack"
Late in the album, on the last verse of this tune, Steve pulls out a cool double-handed 16th-note hi-hat beat with a half-time feel.

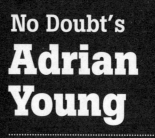

No Doubt's
Adrian Young

Rock Steady

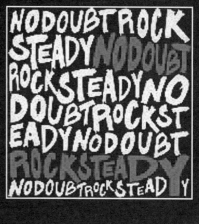

Rock Steady marked No Doubt's return to their exuberant new wave-influenced pop sound, this time splashed with third-world rhythms. Great dance music relies on groove, and groove abounds on this album. Adrian Young provided the human touch amid the various episodes of programming, adding interesting drum beats and flourishes throughout. Here are some examples.

MUSIC KEY

Open H.H. — O   C.C. — ✳
S.D. — (⬤) (⊘) ✕
B.D. — ⬤
Ghost Note | Rim Click

"Hey Baby"
A touch of Caribbean feel from Adrian gives bounce to the chorus and bridge of this hit single.

"Hella Good"
Here's a syncopated snare/bass fill from the middle of this dance tune.

"Underneath It All"
Driving hi-hat accents and four-stroke ruffs bring out the reggae in this half-time groove.

TRACK 47

Adrian throws in some cool triplet fills near the end of the song, with accents and drags playing an important role.

TRACK 48

"Don't Let Me Down"
Here's an unusual repeating pattern from the end of this rocker.

"Start The Fire"
More "island" rhythms show up in the chorus of this tune.

"Rock Steady"
The title track features this wonderful old-school reggae beat by Adrian in the pre-chorus. Note the kick drum placement on 2 and 4.

TRACK 49

The Killers'
Ronnie Vannucci

Hot Fuss

The Killers found the perfect balance between the garage band grind of The Strokes and the pop dance-ability of Duran Duran. But Ronnie Vannucci's drumming displayed a slightly more sophisticated approach than your average post-punk basher. Sprinkled throughout *Hot Fuss* are glimpses of strong drum technique filtered through tasteful restraint. It's a killer combination.

"Jenny Was A Friend Of Mine"

The intro and verse groove from the album's lead track contains a cool little rhythmic twist, shown here at the end of the second measure and continuing into the third. (0:27)

"Mr. Brightside"

Vannucci shows some nice hi-hat control in the classic fast dance beat from this hit single. (0:22)

"Somebody Told Me"

The song that put The Killers on the map features another compelling dance groove. Look at how Ronnie spices up the pattern with his hi-hat work and a Stewart Copeland-esque drum fill at the end of this sequence. (0:45)

TRACK 50

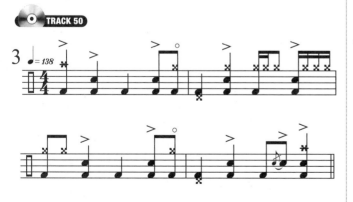

The song climaxes with this great two-bar kick/snare fill. (3:10)

"On Top"

Here's an 8th-note groove from the verse of the tune that has some interesting give-and-take between the kick drum and hi-hat. (0:30)

"Change Your Mind"

This track is loaded with Vannucci's signature snare and bass drum fills, like the following, which leads into the last chorus. (2:41)

"Believe Me Natalie"

Ronnie creates an infectious tom groove at the top of this song, with his snares turned off to add a primal element to the feel. (0:24)

TRACK 51

The chorus beat is just as good, with a nice ride cymbal variation at the top of measure two. (2:22)

TRACK 52

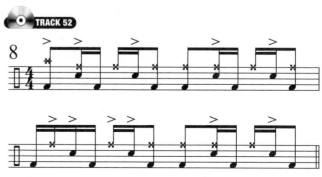

Nirvana's
Dave Grohl
Nevermind

Lissa Wales

As one of the biggest-selling punk rock discs of all time, Nirvana's *Nevermind* helped trigger the alternative rock movement, and it now stands as a bona fide classic. For his part, drummer Dave Grohl supported the tragic brilliance of Kurt Cobain with a mix of hard rock licks, dynamic sensitivity, and a punk basher's attitude. Let's take a close look at some of the details in Grohl's playing on this important record.

"Smells Like Teen Spirit"

This mega-hit contains some of the best drumming on the album. The opening drum fill and groove are as iconic as the song itself. Notice how Grohl throws in alternating snare and hi-hat hits between the bass drum notes in the fill. The drummer also uses a quarter-note hi-hat pattern in the beat, instead of easier-to-play 8th notes. (0:07)

TRACK 53

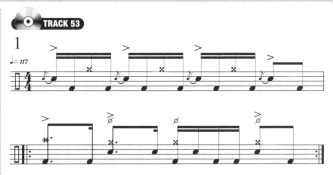

The chorus of a rock anthem needs a proper set-up, and this one is perfect. Dave uses the Keith Moon approach of 8th-note kick drums under a 16th-note snare flourish to provide explosive energy. Then he drops a 16th-note kick in front of a flam to wrap up the fill. (1:04)

In the bridge, Grohl blasts out some cool licks, including a version of his opening fill and a nice triplet move on the toms. (2:44)

"In Bloom"

Here's a particularly John Bonham–esque sequence from Grohl, from the chorus of this tune. The combination of a syncopated kick groove with sweeping 16th note–triplet fills brings to mind the work of the great Zeppelin drummer. (1:02)

"Breed"

Dave specializes in these types of repetitive chorus grooves, and they're almost always unreservedly simple, energetic, and highly effective. (1:07)

"Lithium"

The hit track "Lithium" includes more classic Grohl-isms. This fill features flams and double-stroke kick work, followed by a four-measure pattern containing straightforward beats that are blended together to add rhythmic interest. (0:37)

The chorus beat is a clever bit of invention from Grohl. Dave's bass-flam-bass-flam lick at the end of the second measure allows him to keep his quarter-note hi-hat pattern going through the fill. This enables him to play a beat and a fill at the same time. (1:56)

"Drain You"

The master of the dramatic set-up fill strikes again, this time leading into a pounding groove that drives this track's second verse. (0:47)

"Lounge Act"

Dave plays triplet ruffs around the kit in a couple spots in this song. His clean execution of these tricky licks shows that Grohl could flash chops when needed. This one is an attention-grabbing opening fill. (0:10)

More of the Bonham influence shows up later in the song with this triplet fill. (2:19)

"On A Plain"

The repetition in patterns like this bridge groove reveals how Grohl composes his drum parts like a songwriter. The energy in his performance and the added details keep his drumming sounding fresh. (1:35)

Chapter 3

Metal Masters

Welcome to the dark side! In this chapter we enter a world of speed and power, where ferocious double bass work reigns supreme. The influential Dave Lombardo of Slayer and Lars Ulrich from Metallica lead the way, with new legends being forged by metal veterans Raymond Herrera with Fear Factory, Strapping Young Lad's Gene Hoglan, and Dave McClain with Machine Head. John Dolmayan's System Of A Down, Wuv's P.O.D., and The Rev's Avenged Sevenfold have all crossed into mainstream success, while Joey Jordison's Slipknot and Matt McDonough's Mudvayne bring a performance-art aspect to metal. Each of these players has plenty of chops to burn, as the following pages show.

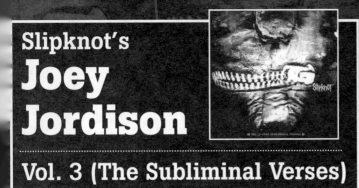

Slipknot's Joey Jordison
Vol. 3 (The Subliminal Verses)

Slipknot's *Vol. 3 (The Subliminal Verses)* found this metal troupe's brand of mayhem flourishing under the guidance of producer-to-the-stars Rick Rubin. Joey Jordison outgunned most of the drumming competition with displays of raw speed and power, contrasted against surprising stretches of restraint when called for. Here are some examples.

"Prelude 3.0"
The dreamy opening track features a subtle beat shift and some nice cymbal work. (0:57)

"The Blister Exists"
The album's first hit contains this interesting marching drum sequence, with the snare part doubled by the band's percussionists. (2:17)

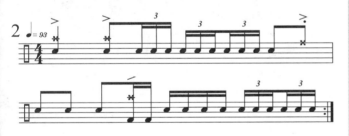

"Three Nil"
Joey's flashy licks shine throughout the album, like the fill setting up the intro of this track. (0:55)

"Opium Of The People"
This quick little seven-beat transition pattern showcases Jordison's ability to place unusual drum and cymbal combinations in furiously fast fills. (0:33)

TRACK 55

"Pulse Of The Maggots"
The pulse of this track is conveyed through a combination of its guitar riff together with this matching drum beat. (1:00)

In the chorus, Joey steers his half-time groove through some compelling rhythm changes. (2:16)

TRACK 56

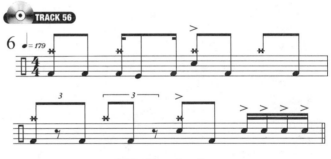

"The Nameless"
It's speed time in this tune, as Jordison's 32nd-note double kick pattern shifts the intro into high gear. (0:20)

TRACK 57

Later in the track, Joey whips out this classic quads lick. (2:41)

TRACK 58

System Of A Down's
John Dolmayan

Steal This Album!

Alex Solca

System Of A Down's *Steal This Album!* is a clean-out-the-closets collection of tracks from the popular nü-metal band's first seven years. For the uninitiated, this compilation was the perfect introduction to John Dolmayan's drumming talents. SOAD's Zappa-like social satire and quirky musical shifts gave John ample opportunity to shine. Let's take a peek at the playing of this powerhouse.

"Innervision"

The intro from this track shows John's mastery of the modern syncopated groove.

TRACK 59

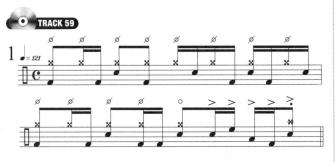

"Bubbles"

This two-minute tune starts in thrash-metal fashion, but then switches to a Middle Eastern feel, complete with a 16th-note tom-tom overdub—and this unusual drum pattern.

TRACK 60

"Nüguns"

Placing the snare on the "&" of the fourth beat in this pattern adds an energetic edge to this song's verse.

"A.D.D."

John's blazing intro beat uses a displaced snare and an offbeat hi-hat pattern to give this tune a disorienting feel.

"I-E-A-I-A-I-O"

John uses this alternating four-bar pattern in the verse of this track. The 16th-note hi-hat beat matches a rapid-fire vocal, while the next two measures support a crunchy guitar riff.

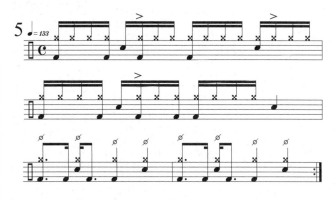

"Highway Song"

This cool fill works its way out of another 16th-note hi-hat groove.

TRACK 61

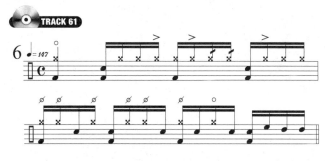

"Thetawaves"

Here's another example of the Dolmayan penchant for alternating patterns. The tension build-up in the paradiddle beat is released in the second measure.

"Streamline"

The frenetic pace of John's groove almost disguises this song's odd time signature.

Metallica's
Lars Ulrich

St. Anger

Courtesy of Tama

St. *Anger,* from metal kings Metallica, was a powerful dissertation on the darker emotions, as raw and pain-filled as an exposed nerve. Lars Ulrich's drum tones were appropriately heavy and slightly distorted, with a ringy snare that sounds, well, *metallic.* Avoiding traditional drum fills, Lars instead weaved each song together with a series of pulsating grooves. Let's examine a few.

"Frantic"

The album abounds with great guitar riffs, and Lars matches each with a compelling beat. This one comes from the intro of the lead track.

In the song's instrumental bridge, Lars pulls out a syncopated half-time groove.

"St. Anger"

The title track contains some vintage Ulrich speed patterns, like these two, from the intro and chorus respectively.

"Some Kind Of Monster"

This beat mirrors James Hetfield's vocal for the first half of the song's verse. Lars then turns up the intensity a bit in the second half by switching some of his bass drum notes to snare.

"My World"

Here's another powerful pattern that punctuates a vocal line. This time it's Hetfield's searing shout, "I don't even know what the question is!"

"Shoot Me Again"

Lars uses splash cymbals and open hi-hat accents to great effect in the verse of this track.

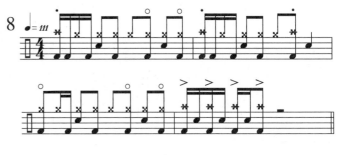

"Purify"

Here are a couple of interesting and unusual grooves. The first is from the 3/4 section of the verse, while the second propels the double-time section.

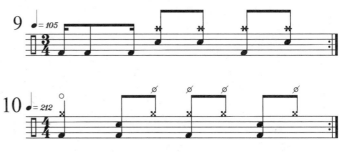

"All Within My Hands"

The first verse of the album's closer features one of Lars' coolest drum beats, which somehow feels like it's moving both fast and slow at the same time.

Alex Solca

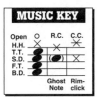
Payable On Death was P.O.D.'s follow-up to their breakthrough album, *Satellite*. Despite a change in guitarists, the band's signature mix of hard rap/metal with soul-searching, uplifting lyrics remained as vibrant as ever. Once again Wuv anchored the rhythm section with his perfectly designed powerful grooves.

"Wildfire"

In the bridge of the opening song, Wuv plays this accented 16th-note snare pattern over quarter notes on the bass drum, contrasting nicely with the heavy groove in the rest of the track. (2:18)

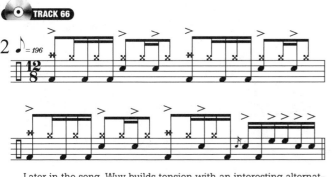

"Will You"

This tune begins with a smooth, flowing 12/8 feel punctuated by well-chosen short fills. (0:05)

TRACK 66

Later in the song, Wuv builds tension with an interesting alternating snare and bass drum pattern. (2:27)

"Change The World"

The intro of this song contains a compelling heavy funk/rock beat. Notice the paradiddle between the kick and snare at the end of the first measure into the beginning of the second. (0:12)

Wuv freestyles a bit with his groove in the tune's verse sections. (0:24)

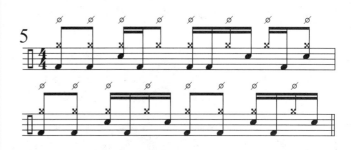

"The Reasons"

The effectiveness of this cool little fill stems from the placement of a snare note on the first beat of the second bar and how that sets up a snare/crash on the second beat of the measure. (1:14)

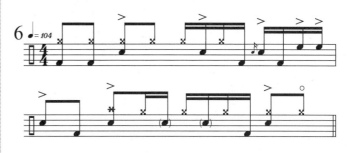

"Waiting On Today"

Here's a classic around-the-kit lick that incorporates some fine bass drum work. (1:53)

TRACK 67

"Eternal"

Check out this unusual offbeat ride cymbal groove from the album's closing track. Wuv uses this pattern to set the mood of the intro before the song's heavy guitars come crashing in. (0:20)

TRACK 68

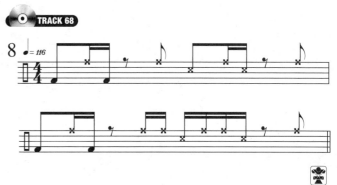

Fear Factory's
Raymond Herrera
Archetype

MUSIC KEY

Raymond Herrera's head-turning double bass technique is clearly evident on Fear Factory's 2004 album, *Archetype*. The band certainly knew they had something special here, as Herrera's kick parts simply dominated the album's mix. Check out some of his patterns, and note the tempos that these grooves are played at.

"Slave Labor"

Making a statement right out of the box, Raymond's intricate bass drum part commands attention in the intro of the opening track. (0:10)

TRACK 69

"Cyberwaste"

Here's another impressive start to a song, as Herrera answers his signature 32nd-note kick flourishes on his snare and tom-tom. (0:00)

The verse then shifts to a classic speed-metal beat—and *speed* is the operative word here. (0:40)

"Act Of God"

The combination of bass drum 16th notes and quarter notes on the snare drives the verse of this song. The change in the bass drum rhythm keeps the pattern interesting. (0:38)

"Drones"

More bunches of speedy 32nd notes on the kick drum show up in the bridge of this tune, along with a nice offset snare pattern. (3:25)

TRACK 70

"Archetype"

This intro uses a moving rhythmic pattern similar to the opening track, albeit in a double-time feel. Raymond matches these types of beats to guitar riffs throughout the album. (0:00)

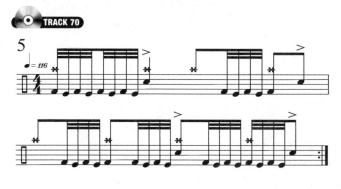

"Bonescraper"

The 6/8 verse of this track gets a dose of Herrera's bass drum magic. (0:24)

TRACK 71

The kick drum onslaught turns relentless as Raymond slams home the song's bridge. His precision on this stuff is astounding! (2:10)

TRACK 72

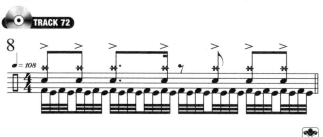

Mudvayne's
Matt McDonough

Lost And Found

The third full-length album from Mudvayne, 2005's *Lost And Found*, saw the boys from Peoria, Illinois stepping out from behind their pseudonyms and stage makeup to create an emotionally honest metal classic. Drummer Matt McDonough's creative and surgically precise patterns are always interesting to explore. So here we go....

"FD"

Throughout the album, Matt constructs disorienting grooves by shifting around his snare patterns, as in this verse beat. (0:30)

TRACK 73

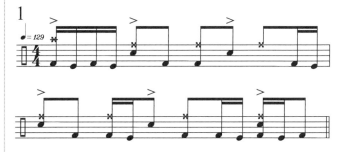

Check out the eye-popping bit of pure speed in this fill from the song's re-intro. (1:58)

"Pushing Through"

McDonough's double kick work is, of course, one of his most effective weapons. Here he uses it to pump energy into a half-time verse. (1:08)

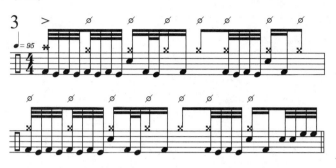

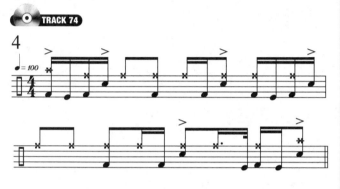

"Happy"

This single features another unique groove with unusual snare placement. (1:16)

TRACK 74

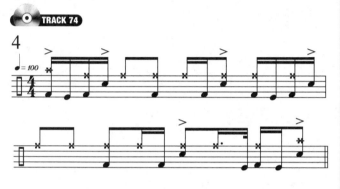

"Rain, Sun, Gone"

Here's Matt using double bass to shove an already intense beat into overdrive. His end fill effectively answers the 32nd-note kick pattern. (3:28)

TRACK 75

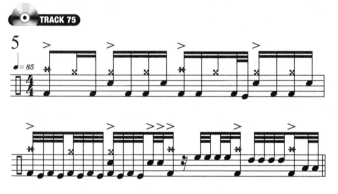

"Choices"

Look at the kick/snare movement in this brilliant little sequence from the climax of this eight-minute opus. The *absence* of McDonough's usual double bass barrage helps keep the attention on the song's important lyrical message. (6:08)

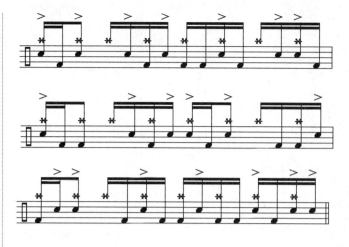

"Just"

The verse of this track contains some great examples of syncopated double kick work in a fast song. (0:23)

"Pulling The String"

Mudvayne flexes their math-rock muscle in this tune. Notice how Matt gives each section of this compound time signature sequence it's own identity by moving from hi-hat to ride cymbal, crash, and finally China cymbal. (0:06)

TRACK 76

Slayer's
Dave Lombardo
Reign In Blood

Alex Solca

If *Reign In Blood* was the only album that Dave Lombardo ever recorded, his place in metal's history would be assured. Over two full decades after its 1986 release, *Reign In Blood* is still considered the pinnacle of thrash metal, evident in its major influence on the death metal movement of the '90s.

Lombardo's innovative style combined incredible energy, strong technique, and killer double bass work to power Slayer's relentless attack. The grooves on *Reign In Blood* influenced scores of modern metal drummers, though few have been able to reach Dave's level of speed, precision, and control. Unlike on many of today's recordings, which are often digitally buffed and polished to perfection, what you hear on this album is exactly what Dave played. Let's have a look at some of the drumming highlights from this important disc.

"Angel Of Death"

The opening track moves through various tempos and feel shifts, but Lombardo saves this all-out rampage for the song's choruses. Check your metronomes on this one. (0:57)

When the song drops into a half-time bridge section, Dave re-enters with a great drum fill. The only interruption in the 32nd-note sticking pattern is a single bass drum note in the first measure. (1:45)

TRACK 77

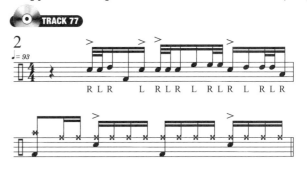

After wild guitar solos by Kerry King and Jeff Hanneman, Lombardo sets up the song's final onslaught with this blazing double bass sequence. Polyrhythm fans will appreciate Dave's quarter note–triplet flams over bass drum 16ths in measure 3. (4:23)

"Piece By Piece"

To build intensity, Lombardo takes two different approaches on this song's intro, changing from cymbal bell triplets... (0:01)

...to a double bass triplet pattern. (0:09)

Later in the track, Dave busts out a short drum solo. His 16th-note double kick beat sets up three different measure-long drum fills, which are each played over an 8th note–triplet guitar riff. (1:20)

"Necrophobic"

Here's a famous beat used by speed metal and hardcore drummers alike. Lombardo's short bursts of 32nd-note fills kick up the energy even higher. (0:05)

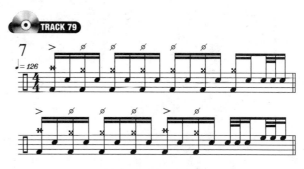

"Raining Blood"

The album's closer is another thrash metal opus, complete with an eerie-sounding instrumental intro, various changing tempos, and Lombardo's double bass barrage. This classic groove sets up the song's first verse. (0:45)

After a fiery thrash section, the track's half-time chorus features this punchy double-kick beat. (2:39)

Finally, the song erupts into howling guitar solos for the album's most wired sequence. Dave holds it together, while managing to squeeze in short machine-gun fills as the band careens towards a thunderstorm finish. (2:53)

Reign In Blood is thirty minutes of pure metal mayhem, containing more energy and attitude than most albums twice its length. Through it all, Dave Lombardo is the driving force, never out of control but always pushing the band to new extremes. It's a masterful performance.

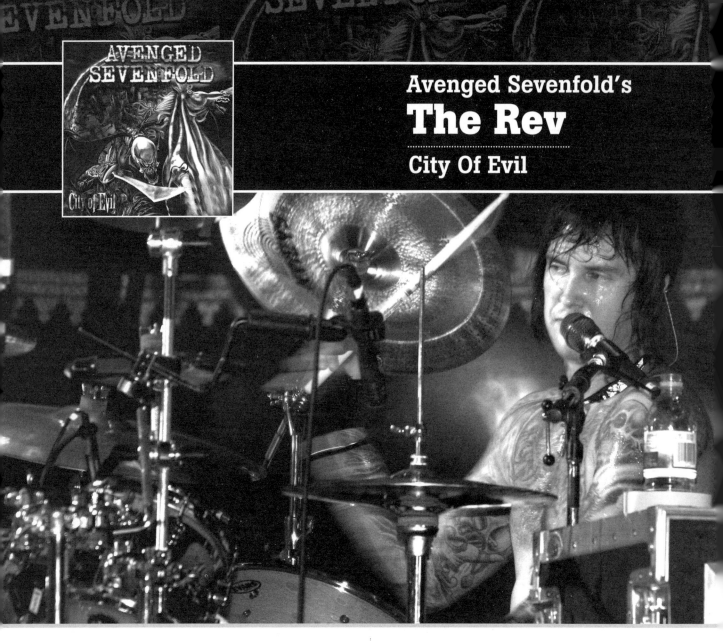

Avenged Sevenfold's
The Rev
City Of Evil

MUSIC KEY

Times were good for Avenged Sevenfold in 2005. A prime spot on the Warped Tour and plenty of radio airplay led to national exposure and big sales for the metal band's major-label debut. Underscoring this Southern California quintet's mixture of heavy guitar harmonies and intricate arrangements was a crackling rhythm section, featuring James "The Rev" Sullivan on drums.

The Rev's grooves are solid and upfront on *City Of Evil,* and fans of hardcore drumming will enjoy the drummer's rapid-fire single strokes and double-kick combinations. Here are a few highlights.

"Beast And The Harlot"
The Rev gets a featured spot on the disc's first track with the following four-bar drum solo. He blasts through two- and four-note tradeoffs with a nice sense of phrasing and plenty of speed to burn. (3:32)

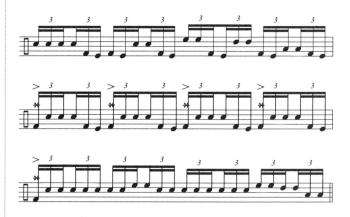

"Burn It Down"
This song begins with a percussive guitar riff that The Rev matches on his snare drum while using double kicks to fill in the holes in the rhythm. In the second four measures, he builds tension by changing to continuous 16th notes in his bass drums. (0:00)

TRACK 80

$\downarrow$ = 155

2

"Blinded In Chains"

"Blinded In Chains" also opens with a staccato guitar/drum riff. Once again, The Rev adds nonstop kick drums in the second four bars before catapulting into a driving quarter-note groove. (0:00)

3

After a furious cut-time section with a double lead guitar solo, the song finally settles into a verse. During this section, The Rev plays a few more double bass notes to keep things moving along. (1:00)

4

When the band returns to the intro riff, The Rev has another brief solo spot. This one showcases an intricate and impressive double bass figure in the third and fourth measures. (2:50)

5

"Bat Country"

This hit single features a double-time groove (shown in the first measure below). The Rev ramps up the intensity at the end of the verse by playing 16ths between snare and bass drum (measure 2). He then adds his left foot, turning the rhythm into 16th-note triplets (measure 3). Finally, the phrase climaxes with double kick triplets that help ease the transition into the chorus's slower tempo. (0:32)

TRACK 81

6

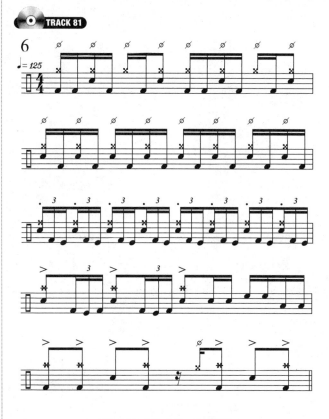

"Trashed And Scattered"

Here's a slow, heavy groove from an interlude that occurs near the end of "Trashed And Scattered." This section gives The Rev a chance to have fun with an old-school metal double kick part. (4:23)

TRACK 82

7

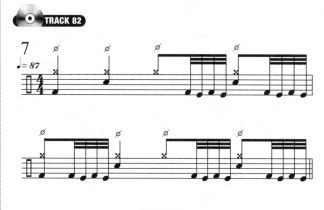

"M.I.A."

The tempo jumps back up for the album's last song. This track features a galloping beat under a quarter-note bell pattern. Double bass figures like this add plenty of drive to the music without the clutter of continuous 16th notes. (4:41)

8

Strapping Young Lad's
Gene Hoglan
The New Black

Gene Ambo

Look out, metalheads. Strapping Young Lad's *The New Black* gave drummer Gene Hoglan ample opportunity to ply his power and skill with more adrenaline-pumping patterns. The following grooves are just the tip of the iceberg.

"Decimator"

On the opening track, Gene tosses in two 16th notes on the first beat to break up the unrelenting triplets of Devin Townsend and Jed Simon's guitar riffs. (0:31)

"U Suck"

Here, Hoglan intensifies his blast beat with a speedy double-bass quad at the end of each phrase. (0:27)

"Monument"

Hoglan has a knack for inverting drum patterns. In this track, he reverses the kick and snare placement in the second two measures. The result is that the first pattern grooves, while the second one *slams*. (0:24)

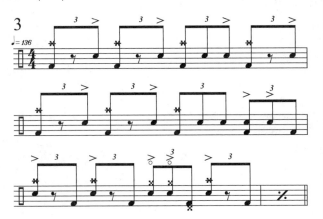

"Wrong Side"

The album's first single explodes with a terrific double kick opening. Snare/hi-hat unison 16ths give way to syncopated accents that follow the song's guitar riff, while 32nd-note kicks keep blasting away. For the verse, the groove shifts to the upbeats, with some occasional double kicks to push things along. (0:00)

"Hope"

The chorus groove from this slow and heavy track is a lesson in effective beat design. Hoglan's simple rhythm on beats 1 and 4 accent the band's chord changes, while triplets on beats 2 and 3 underscore

Devin Townsend's screamed vocal message. Gene switches between two crash cymbals for further emphasis. (1:06)

Later in the song, Hoglan uses triplets to punctuate the chord change accents (measures 1–2), followed by a continuous double-kick bombardment. (2:58)

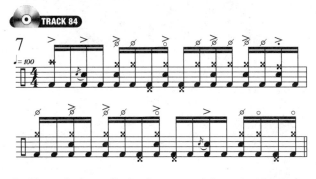

"Almost Again"

During the verse of this tune, Gene shows off his incredible single bass technique. He employs steady 16ths with his right foot, while using the left to drop in some open and closed hi-hat accents. (0:00)

In the song's chorus, Hoglan demonstrates that a short burst of double kick can be just as effective as a non-stop barrage. (1:28)

"The New Black"

The title track revolves around an ominous 16th note–triplet guitar riff, which Gene propels with a powerful groove. The openness of the quarter-note crash pattern provides extra drive while keeping the beat uncluttered. (0:35)

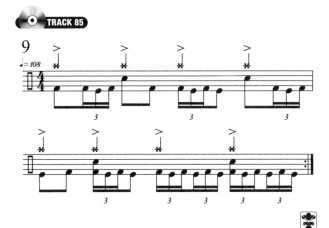

Machine Head's
Dave McClain
The Blackening

MUSIC KEY

M achine Head's *The Blackening* is filled with earth-scorching vocals and ferocious guitar riffs, all propelled by the strong drumming of Dave McClain. In-your-face double bass dominated, but McClain didn't slather it on with reckless abandon. Instead, he found creative ways for his double kicks to enhance the music. Here are some highlights.

"Clenching The Fists Of Dissent"

The disc's ten-minute opening track moves through various moods and tempos. Dave's groove for the half-time chorus contrasts double bass with open space. Notice how the triplet fill at the end of bar 2 becomes the rhythmic theme in measures 3 and 4. (2:56)

TRACK 86

Later in the track, the band erupts into a frantic thrash riff. (5:49)

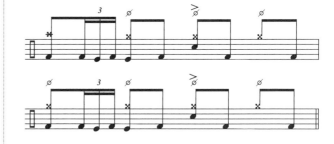

"Beautiful Mourning"

This four-bar chorus pattern shows McClain using double bass to spice up a section without trampling over it. The fill in the last measure is a cool touch. (1:04)

3

"Aesthetics Of Hate"

Dave mirrors this song's percussive guitar riff with his own 32nd- and 16th-note combination. The space in the second and fourth beats allows the groove to breathe. (1:49)

4

McClain switches to a 16th note–triplet kick pattern in a climatic section of this track. (3:52)

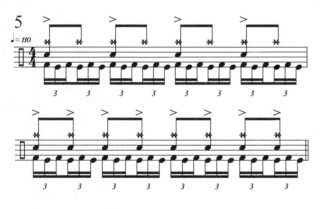

5

"Now I Lay Thee Down"

This heavy 6/8 groove divides 16th notes into groups of three and two. Dave ends this section with some quads around the kit. (3:20)

TRACK 87

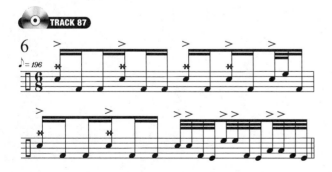

6

"Slanderous"

McClain's sparse beat in the half-time intro of this heavy shuffle allows the triplet guitar riff to carry the section. The double-kick flourish in measure 4 really stands out against the open groove. (0:17)

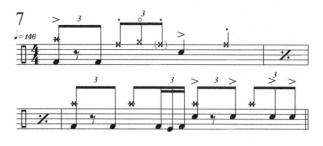

7

"Halo"

Here's a slow, grinding groove that's loaded with 16th- and 32nd-note kicks. (1:02)

TRACK 88

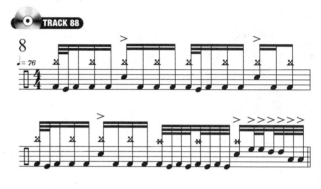

8

"Wolves"

McClain's quarter-note snare pattern helps anchor this foot-heavy chorus groove. (1:08)

TRACK 89

9

"A Farewell To Arms"

Before the album's closer turns ultra-heavy, McClain delivers this compelling pattern in the chorus. The reoccurring tom figures add tonal variety to the beat. (3:37)

10

Chapter 4

Funk's Finest

Funk music demands the ultimate combination of technique and pocket, and the group of players featured in this chapter provide that and more. From the intricate syncopations of Carter Beauford and the explosive Dennis Chambers to the straight-up funk of Soulive's Alan Evans and The Chili Peppers' Chad Smith, these drummers make the music *feel* good. Pros like The Roots' ?uestlove and Primus's Tim Alexander creatively bounce between the simple and complex. Session master Steve Jordan brings his impeccable sound to The John Mayer Trio. And for a slightly different perspective, included are a couple of singing stars who happen to also be first-rate funk drummers: Lenny Kravitz and the immortal Stevie Wonder. It's time to groove with a capital G!

Lenny Kravitz

Greatest Hits

This multi-platinum CD covers over ten years of retro funk/rock hits from Lenny's first five albums. The one new track included, "Again," was also a major smash. While his live show featured other drummers, in the studio Lenny lays down his own grooves. And who can blame him? This stuff has *got* to be fun to play.

"Are You Gonna Go My Way"
Here's the fill and beat coming out of the guitar solo in this driving riff-rocker.

"Fly Away"
Lenny loves slow, funky grooves. A slight accent in the 16th-note hi-hat pattern punctuates the end of each guitar riff.

TRACK 90

"Rock And Roll Is Dead"
Here's a wonderful four-bar sequence from the verse of this tune. Notice how the snare drum ghost notes in bars three and four add depth to the groove.

TRACK 91

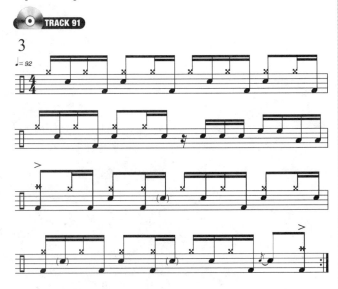

"Again"
A slap echo on the drum track enhances the slow, heavy feel of this tune. Lenny plays it simple and powerful, with the song's only fill kicking things off.

"It Ain't Over Till It's Over"
Another 16th-note funk groove, with an occasional fill to spice things up.

"American Woman"
Lenny keeps the tension up in this track by never bringing in a snare drum backbeat.

"Always On The Run"
Here's the opening fill and groove from this guitar-driven cut, as well as its chorus pattern.

TRACK 92

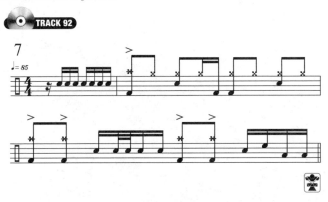

The Dave Matthews Band's
Carter Beauford
Busted Stuff

MUSIC KEY

Busted Stuff, was a return to form for both The Dave Matthews Band and its drummer Carter Beauford. This one has all of the classic Beauford-isms: the relaxed yet intense fat back-beat grooves, the idiosyncratic hi-hat work, and the explosive tom fills. It's time for another schooling from one of rock's finest.

"Busted Stuff"

The opening bars of the lead track showcase a new duality in Carter's playing: sparseness in the first measure followed by a busy pattern in the next. The 16th notes are slightly swung in this one.

"Grey Street"

Here's a typically incredible sequence from Carter, leading into the second verse in this song. This stuff just seems to flow out of him.

TRACK 93

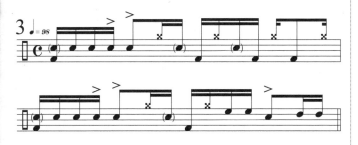

"Where Are You Going"

This nice little chorus groove works best with the left stick playing the hi-hat pattern.

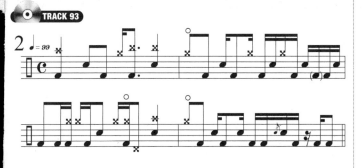

"You Never Know"

In this song, Carter plays a Cuban-style ride cymbal rhythm following the first chorus, then launches back into the verse with a syncopated fill that bypasses the downbeat of the following measure.

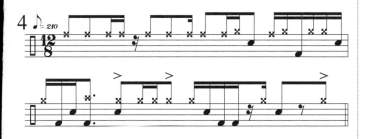

"Captain"

Here's a perfect example of Carter's penchant for turning the beat around by slipping into his linear style in the middle of an otherwise straightforward funk groove.

TRACK 94

"Kit Kat Jam"

This instrumental in 3/4 time gives Carter a chance to step out with one of his favorite 32nd-note licks.

"Digging A Ditch"

Check out this head-turning sequence from the CD's slowest track.

TRACK 95

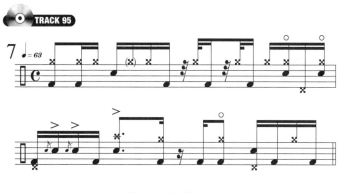

"Bartender"

Finally, here's a look at a marching groove from the album closer, featuring some of Carter's delicate roll technique.

The Classic Grooves Of
Stevie Wonder

During Stevie Wonder's peak years as a recording artist, it seemed as if he could do no wrong. Between 1972 and 1976 he released some of the greatest R&B albums of all time, much of which he created with little help from other musicians.

A brilliant multi-instrumentalist, Stevie's drumming represents just a fraction of his immense talent. Compared to his songwriting, singing, keyboard and harmonica playing, and musical innovations, his drumming is often overlooked. We pay tribute to one of America's finest musicians by putting the spotlight directly on his percussive abilities. Here are some of his best drum grooves from throughout his recording career.

Music Of My Mind (1972)
"Love Having You Around"

Stevie Wonder had a great early career in the '60s as a child star at Motown, where he learned the art of making records from the label's legendary musicians and producers. This album marked his artistic coming of age. With the exception of a few solos by guest musicians, the entire album was written, produced, and performed by Stevie. In this opening funk track, check out how he returns to 8th notes on the hi-hat halfway through the second bar. (3:33)

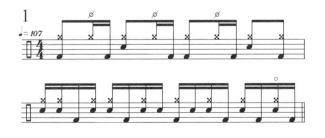

"Seems So Long"

This half-time ballad is even more jazz-flavored. The interplay between Stevie's ride cymbal, hi-hat, and bass drum reveals impressive coordination and technique. (1:17)

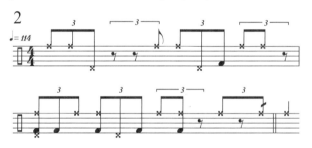

Talking Book (1972)
"You Are The Sunshine Of My Life"

Talking Book was Stevie's commercial breakthrough. Its release signaled the beginning of a five-year stretch of success that made him one of the most dominant artists of the era. This tune became a pop standard. It begins as a gentle love song before erupting with an energy provided mostly by Wonder's drumming. Notice the ride cymbal/kick drum interplay in this chorus beat. (2:12)

"Superstition"

Here's one of the coolest drum intros of all time. The infectious feel of this groove comes directly from the swing in Stevie's hi-hat work. (0:00)

TRACK 96

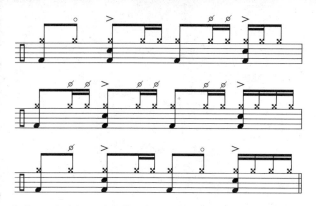

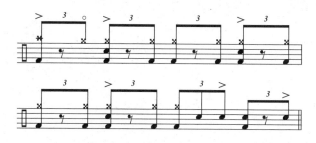

At the end of the song's first chorus, Stevie plays the following drum break, which perfectly encapsulates his unique combination of strong technique and uninhibited style. (1:13)

Fulfillingness' First Finale (1974)
"It Ain't No Use"

Wonder's next album continued to deliver hits. In the ending chorus of this track, Stevie pulls off some great ride cymbal work with bell accents while moving his snare off of the usual backbeats. (3:08)

Innervisions (1973)
"Too High"

Stevie's follow-up to *Talking Book*, *Innervisions*, is another leap forward with a strong turn towards social commentary. The album opens with this great funk groove. Check out the double-stroke/ghost-note combinations in his hi-hat triplets. (0:02)

Songs In The Key Of Life (1976)
"Knocks Me Off My Feet"

For the album that many fans feel is his greatest achievement, Stevie employed a full band of musicians for some important tracks. (Drummer Raymond Pounds drums on "Sir Duke" and "I Wish.") However, Wonder's unique drumming graces much of the album. On this song, his playful 16th-note cymbal pattern sounds like it was placed on the bell of the hi-hat. In bar 2, note the two offbeat open hi-hats over a straight bass drum part. (0:09)

"Living For The City"

Here's Wonder's 3/4 drum solo that occurs just before the famous breakdown in this song. The repeating triplet ruffs provide a rhythmic theme as well as the perfect jump-off point into each lick. (3:55)

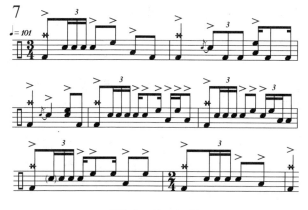

In the final chorus groove, Stevie's bass drum and syncopated hi-hat patterns reveal another tricky coordination move. (2:43)

"Summer Soft"

At the end of this track, Stevie is jamming full-out, with multiple fills and funky grooves performed in his inimitable style. (3:23)

"Higher Ground"

The opening shuffle groove for this hit accompanies Stevie's wah-wah clavinet riff. Note how he doubles the bass drum with the hi-hat. (0:06)

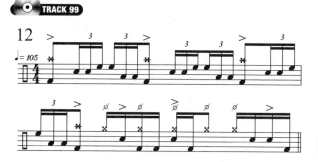

The Roots' Questlove's Soulful Grooves

MUSIC KEY

The Roots' album, *The Tipping Point*, is further evidence of ?uestlove's king-of-the-hill status in the hip-hop drumming world. The album's grooves virtually defy you to keep still, as ?uestlove propels the songs with his understated yet compelling rhythms. Let's take a look at some of those grooves, as well as a few from The Tipping Point's predecessor, *Phrenology*, and from ?uestlove's side project, The Philadelphia Experiment.

The Tipping Point
"I Don't Care"

?uestlove strikes the perfect balance between the volume of his ghost notes and the intensity of the backbeat in this groove. The slight change in the bass drum part and the single open hi-hat add interest. (0:00)

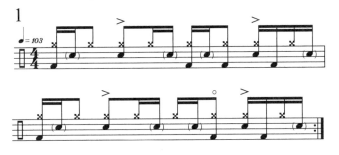

"Guns Are Drawn"

The staccato 8th-note feel of this pattern sets the bed for rapper Black Thought's 16th-note delivery. ?uestlove drops one 16th-note bass drum pickup into the first bar to release the 8th-note tension. (0:03)

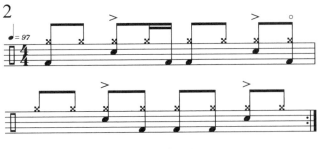

"Stay Cool"

Here's another example of the effectiveness of a relaxed 8th-note beat under a 16th-note rhythmic vocal, with a hint of 16th groove in the hi-hat part. (0:06)

"Web"

The strength of this beat lies in the offbeat ride cymbal pattern (with every other note landing on the bell), combined with swung ghost notes. If this groove doesn't make you bob your head, you've got problems. (0:00)

"Boom!"

The Clyde Stubblefield-inspired left-hand work is the key to this incredible beat. ?uestlove combines the rimshot on beat 2 with a flurry of ghost notes and a well-placed accented drag. (0:18)

TRACK 100

"Why (What's Goin' On?)"

Near the end of the album, a freestyle drums and vocal jam ensues, giving ?uestlove a chance to bring some licks to the table. Here are a couple of cool sequences. (10:11 and 10:19)

Phrenology

"The Seed"

The accented hi-hats elevate this driving drumbeat. (1:11)

"Break You Off"

The end of this single explodes into a great drum 'n' bass–style section, with ?uestlove pushing the boundaries of syncopated drumming. (4:58)

TRACK 101

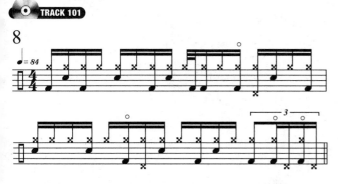

"Something In The Way Of Things (In Town)"

Here's more syncopation, this time in a free-flowing ride cymbal groove with a jazzier flavor. (2:05)

The Philadelphia Experiment

"Philadelphia Experiment"

?uestlove employs his drum 'n' bass chops in the opening track from this jazz/funk release. Note his slick left-hand snare drum work. (0:55)

TRACK 102

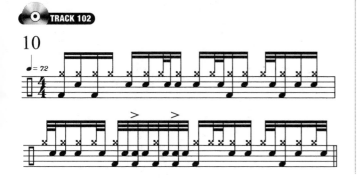

"Grover"

There's more left-hand magic in the placement of the swung ghost notes in this smooth groove. (0:14)

"Call For All Demons"

This one's all about open and closed hi-hats, with ?uestlove weaving them in and out of the turned-around drumbeat. (2:45)

TRACK 103

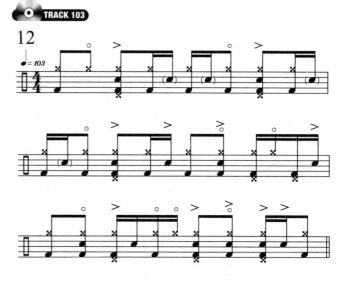

"Ain't It The Truth"

This album gives ?uestlove plenty of opportunity to stretch out and improvise on great funk patterns, like this one. (1:05)

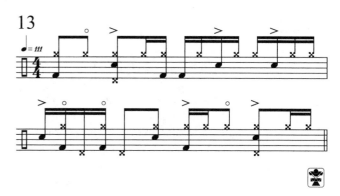

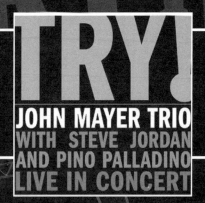

John Mayer Trio's
Steve Jordan

Try!

Sporting monster guitar chops and a blues/rock sound, John Mayer elevated his status from heartthrob singer/songwriter to serious musical heavyweight with his eye-opening album *Try!* Joining him for this transformation was the to-die-for rhythm section of bassist Pino Palladino and top session drummer Steve Jordan.

Jordan is in peak form on this live recording, laying down incredible grooves under Mayer's soulful songs. With a loose yet unwavering feel, Steve sets each track deep in the pocket with a mix of funky patterns and straight-ahead beats. Here are some examples.

"Who Did You Think I Was"

Steve's opening fill on the album's first track contains a barely audible six-stroke roll that leads into rimshot accents. From there, Jordan's turned-around groove keeps things moving under Mayer's bluesy guitar riff. (0:21)

TRACK 104

"Good Love Is On The Way"

The guitar solo section of this song features a syncopated groove with accented offbeats on the ride cymbal. (2:40)

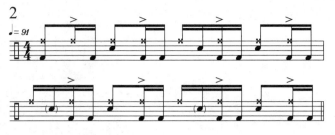

"Wait Until Tomorrow"

How can you hope to match Mitch Mitchell's drumming magic when covering a Jimi Hendrix classic? Jordan circumvents the challenge by creating one of his most outlandishly funky grooves for Mayer's version of this tune. Check it out: This is one killer beat. (0:09)

TRACK 105

"Another Kind Of Green"

Steve swings the feel of this 12/8 track by placing his ghost notes and offbeats as far behind the beat as he can. The splashy 8th notes on the ride are further defined by being doubled with the left foot. (0:07)

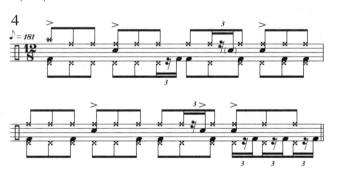

"I Got A Woman"

Jordan's beat for Mayer's cover of this Ray Charles song is a testament to the effectiveness of ghost notes. With incredible left-hand control, Steve places his rimshots and ghost notes at opposite ends of

the dynamic spectrum. This groove is so strong that Mayer has the drummer open the song by himself. (0:09)

TRACK 106

"Something's Missing"

Jordan starts this tune with another unaccompanied groove. The deep pulse of the accented hi-hat pattern, combined with well-placed ghost notes, is what makes this beat feel so good. (0:00)

"Try"

The title track is a lively R&B rave up that closes the album. Steve provides forward momentum with a barking hi-hat part in the verses. (0:51)

Jordan augments his groove with more snare and kick drum offbeats when he changes to the ride cymbal for Mayer's guitar solo. (2:13)

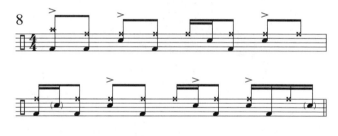

Finally, Steve goes all-out for the end of the song. His overdriven drumbeat is an energetic and effective show-closer. (4:59)

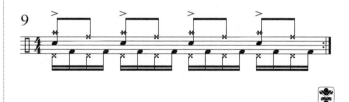

Dennis Chambers
Boston T Party

Cooking up great funk grooves comes naturally to Dennis Chambers, and this disc showcased that side of his playing while the rest of the band provided fiery solos on top. Along the way Dennis slipped in some tasty licks to spice things up. Here are a few samples.

"D'funk'd"

The album opens with a mid-tempo funk tune that Chambers underplays to focus the attention on his bandmates. Late in the track, the groove switches to a marching-style snare beat during which Dennis eases in some nice double strokes and accents over a splashing hi-hat pattern. (4:22)

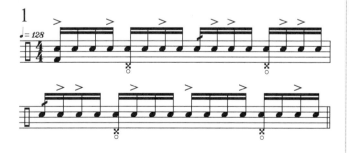

"(Great) Ball Of Issues"

This New Orleans–flavored cut starts with the following four-bar drum intro. Chambers' relaxed approach sets the tone for the track, as he flows through rolls and accents with the easy feel that the genre requires. Notice how well his kick and hi-hat placement augments the second-line snare groove. (0:00)

TRACK 107

Several bars into the song, this five-stroke roll sequence alternating between hi-hat and snare (starting on the last beat of the first measure below) is a real attention grabber. (0:47)

"Around About Way"

On the album's uptempo third track, Dennis uses a charging open hi-hat pattern and some speedy fills to push things forward. (0:58)

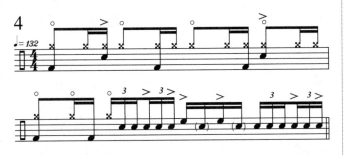

Halfway into the tune, the bass and guitar drop out, leaving Chambers to support T Lavitz's extended keyboard solo. This quickly becomes more of a duet, as Dennis plays off of the rhythms in Lavitz's riffs. Look at the bass drum work in the first two measures of this four-bar section. (2:30)

Finally, the piece moves into a section featuring David Fiuczynski soloing over a James Brown–style groove. Dennis does a spot-on Clyde Stubblefield impersonation here. (3:29)

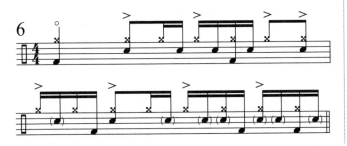

"All Thought Out"

This tune starts out as a jazz ballad and then takes a left turn into a sweet samba groove. Check out the beautiful snare and cymbal interplay in this two-bar excerpt. (2:44)

"Deff 184"

This track segues out of another song via Jeff Berlin's frantic, funky bass line. The left-hand work in Chambers' accompanying beat is astounding at this speed. (0:00)

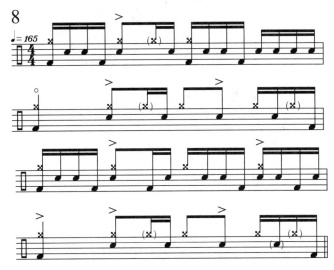

"Constant Comment"

Late in the album the groove turns jazzier, giving Dennis a chance to stretch out in a more free-flowing style. Here he alternates splashing hi-hats with snare/cymbal double strokes. (0:09)

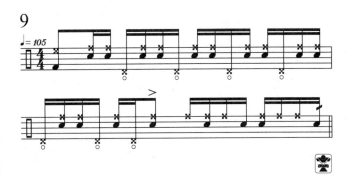

Primus's Tim Alexander

They Can't All Be Zingers

Primus is one of the most unusual bands to find mainstream success. Borderline punk/funk, with a healthy dose of a Rush influence and Frank Zappa–like humor thrown in, Primus's music showcases the instrumental talents of bassist/leader Les Claypool and drummer Tim Alexander.

Each Primus track is built around bizarre vocals and percussive bass sounds, and Tim Alexander's drumming takes on an almost conversational dialog with Claypool's parts. Quirky beats, explosive fills, and solid timekeeping—Alexander employs it all in his work with Primus. Here's a sampling of his playing from the band's 2006 best-of release.

"To Defy The Laws Of Tradition"

This track opens with a bass solo. Alexander's entrance fill embellishes a few accents with Claypool, and then yanks the listener into a great funk groove designed around heavy accents on beats 3 and 4 of each measure. (0:52)

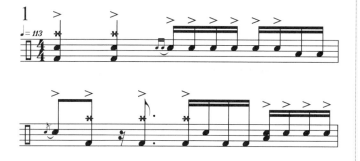

"John The Fisherman"

Tim's double kick drum work is always tasty. Here's a cool lick from this song's chorus. (1:48)

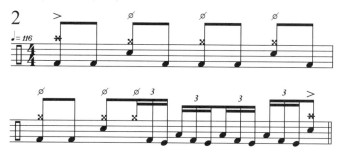

"Too Many Puppies"

Alexander gets to step out a bit in this four-bar solo. While the majority of the sequence features a loose hi-hat, notice how Tim changes to a closed hi-hat to focus attention on his 32nd-note kicks in bars one and three. (3:29)

3

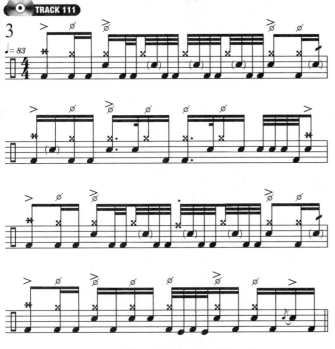

"Jerry Was A Race Car Driver"

The bridge of this quirky hit simulates the intensity and chaos of a car race. Claypool shouts "Go!" and shifts into overdrive as Tim switches to his China cymbal to drive home the groove over double bass flourishes. (1:36)

4

"Tommy The Cat"

The opening two-bar drum fill of this song demonstrates how accents, ghost notes, drags, and flams can elevate a simple idea into something special. Tim accelerates the tempo as the fill moves along so that things are jumping when he kicks into his funk groove. (0:00)

5

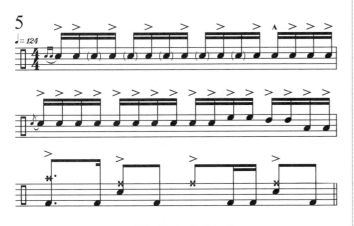

"My Name Is Mud"

One of Primus's most famous tunes hangs on Claypool's triplet bass lick. After providing straightforward beat support with a few accents thrown in, Alexander finally plays along with the pattern for the climax of the song. The depth of his low tom (which is actually a gong bass) completes the triple-bass effect. (4:11)

6

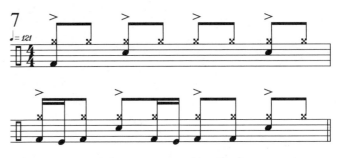

"DMV"

Tim's use of space in the first measure of this verse groove enhances the impact of his double bass pattern in bar two. (0:20)

7

"Over The Electric Grapevine"

For this track, Alexander applies a tom-laden, almost tribal approach. His drumbeat under Larry LaLonde's guitar solo, with offbeat cymbals mixed into the tom work, is an example of Tim's fluent creativity. (2:24)

8

"Wynona's Big Brown Beaver"

Tim's flashy double bass triplets pump energy into the groove of this song. Occasional fills burst out of the beat to add excitement. (0:20)

9

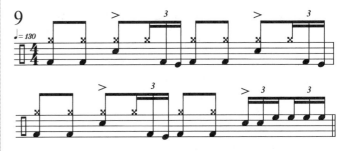

"Southbound Pachyderm"

The end of this cut finds Alexander going a little nuts with Neil Peart–inspired licks. Note the smooth integration of double kick and ride cymbal into the sweeping tom fill at the end of this sequence. (4:55)

10

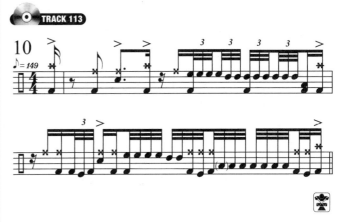

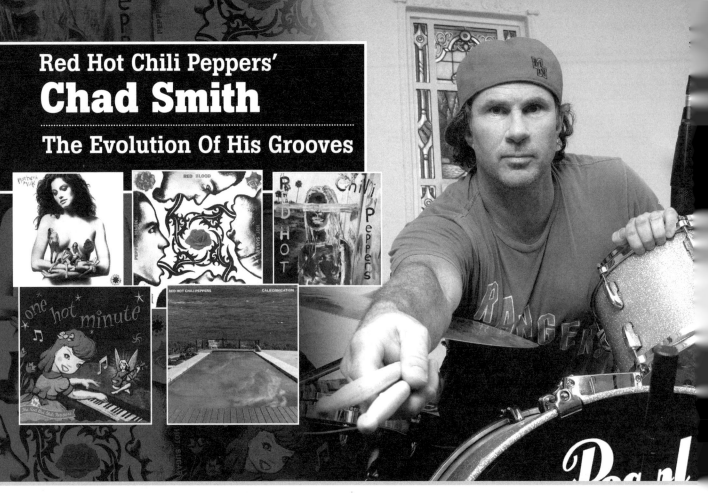

Red Hot Chili Peppers' Chad Smith
The Evolution Of His Grooves

It's hard to imagine a more perfect drummer for The Red Hot Chili Peppers than Chad Smith. Fate brought them together in 1988, when the Chili Peppers were a regionally popular punk/funk band out of Southern California with a reputation for wild stage shows and a few innovative but largely undiscovered albums under their belt.

After the loss of a couple of members, the band found new guitarist John Frusciante and began the long search for the right drummer. "We auditioned about fifty thousand drummers and hired Chad Smith," says bassist Flea in the liner notes of the re-mastered *Mother's Milk* album. "Chad sat down at the drums and lit a fire under our asses...he could play drums on anything."

Indeed, finding Chad Smith was fortunate for the band. Drummers with enough power to handle the slamming hard edge of rock and punk, while possessing the skills and finesse to create compelling funk grooves, are few and far between. Chad's taste, versatility, and technical ability became invaluable ingredients in the band's developing sound.

As the band's music has evolved over the years, so too has Smith's drumming. But he always finds the perfect groove for each situation. Let's take a look back through Chad's Chili Peppers catalog and highlight some of his best grooves.

Mother's Milk (1989)
Chad's first album with the Chili Peppers became the band's breakthrough, gaining MTV exposure for the hits "Higher Ground" and "Knock Me Down." The two tracks included here (Examples 1 and 2) sound as if they were written around Chad's dominating drum beats. The funky "Subway To Venus" groove contains an interesting snare/kick note at the end, while "Magic Johnson" switches between a unique trainbeat and a driving marching pattern.

"Subway To Venus" (0:00)

"Magic Johnson" (0:14 & 0:28)

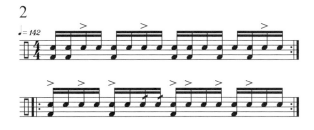

Blood Sugar Sex Magik (1991)
The band changed record labels and producers for their next release, which spawned the mega-hits "Under The Bridge," "Breaking The Girl," and "Give It Away." This album remains the Chili Peppers' all-time best-seller. Rick Rubin's stripped-down production brought out the details in the drumming, and Chad capitalized with some incredible grooves. Check out the ghost-note work in

"If You Have To Ask," and the flowing 6/8 pattern of the haunting single "Breaking The Girl." Then it's back to the *funk* with one of Smith's greatest grooves, the swing-feel ghost-note magic of "Mellowship Slinky In B Major."

"If You Have To Ask" (0:20)

TRACK 114

"Breaking The Girl" (0:54)

"Mellowship Slinky In B Major" (0:25)

TRACK 115

One Hot Minute (1995)

Not long after *Blood Sugar Sex Magik* was released, guitarist John Frusciante left the group. This led the Chili Peppers to bring in Jane's Addiction guitarist Dave Navarro. Navarro's heavy-hitting approach took the band in a more metal direction, pulling Chad back to his days as a straightforward slammer. Despite this change, *One Hot Minute* contains some great drum patterns. Chad's syncopated beat for "Warped" adheres to Navarro's guitar riff like a second skin, and the bouncy offbeat groove of "Deep Kick" is a coordination challenge that features some nice snare work and an 8th-note left-foot hi-hat pattern that keeps the energy driving.

"Warped" (0:48)

"Deep Kick" (1:45)

TRACK 116

Californication (1999)

Dave Navarro's stint in the Chili Peppers lasted for only one album. With guitarist John Frusciante back in the fold, fans had high hopes for a return to the band's earlier sound. And coming off like the real follow-up to *Blood Sugar Sex Magik*, *Californication* didn't disappoint. The funkiness that had been downplayed on much of *One Hot Minute* was restored, which meant that Chad was in his element again. His beat for the title track contains subtle left-hand work, while "I Like Dirt" features one of his all-time funkiest beats. And "Right On Time" shows that the inner punk is still present.

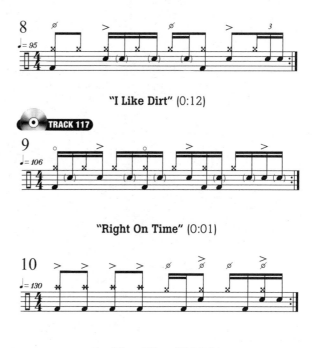

"Californication" (0:16)

"I Like Dirt" (0:12)

TRACK 117

"Right On Time" (0:01)

By The Way (2002)

Having recaptured their crown as alt-funk kings with *Californication*, The Red Hot Chili Peppers designed their next release to showcase their soulful pop/rock side without dulling the band's edge. *By The Way* turns the focus to melody and harmony, and Chad Smith's drumming is right in step with this new approach. This album features stripped-down grooves that propel each song without unnecessary clutter. When called upon, Chad's energy still drives the band (as in his great tom groove for the rap section of the title track). But his simple beat for the guitar-led funk of "Can't Stop" shows how he selflessly plays for the song.

"By The Way" (0:35)

"Can't Stop" (0:32)

Soulive's
Alan Evans
Break Out

W. Churgin

Soulive's *Break Out* album took a step away from the jazz-funk trio's previous jam-band approach and moved towards classic instrumental R&B. The album's leaner, tighter compositions also included a few top-notch vocal songs from guest stars like Ivan Neville, Chaka Khan, and Reggie Watts. Grooves are pushed to the forefront here, with drummer Alan Evans giving a virtual clinic on the art of understated funk drumming. Below are some of his best patterns from *Break Out*.

"Reverb"

Alan lays back the offbeats in his bass drum pattern as far as he can to deepen the pocket in this compelling groove. (0:02)

1

"Got Soul"

This one's all about the ghost notes. Evans applies the perfect dynamic to blend them into his 8th-note hi-hat pattern. (0:05)

2

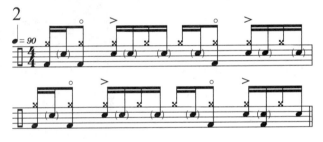

"Cachaca"

Alan's kick drum pattern in this Latin-tinged track locks in with his brother Neal's keyboard bass line. (0:04)

3

"Break Out"

Alan's knack for adding just a touch of swing to his playing contributes strongly to the overall feel of the album. Here, he applies it to his bass drum part. (0:00)

4

"Crosstown Traffic"

Soulive's rave-up rendition of this Jimi Hendrix classic gives guitarist Eric Krasno a chance to work out with guest pedal steel guitarist Robert Randolph. Alan's funked-up take on Mitch Mitchell's drum part adds to the excitement. (0:32)

5

"Take It Easy"

Again, the placement of Evans' kick drum offbeats establishes the groove in the intro of this funky track. (0:05)

6

In the song's verse, Alan shifts the emphasis over to his snare drum, using three different dynamics (accent, non-accent, and ghost note) to carry the groove. The way these patterns interact with Neal's bass lines and the band's horn section is magical. (0:23)

7

"Vapor"

Alan comes out of the middle breakdown section of this track with an explosive fill. The subsequent deep groove results from snare drum ghost notes contrasted against heavy downbeat hi-hat accents. (3:44)

TRACK 118

8

"Interlude III"

This cool album closer contains the disc's strangest drum beat. And no, the 8th-note hi-hat at the end of the second measure is not a typo! (0:23)

TRACK 119

9

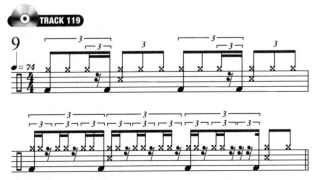

Chapter 5

Wizards Of Prog

Here's where the true technicians reside. Prog's odd time signatures and rhythms require creativity, control, and chops, all of which are in abundance among this collection of drummers. Our look back to the early masters of the genre spotlights Bill Bruford's work with Yes and Phil Collins' with Genesis.

Popular modern practitioners included here are Dominic Howard with Muse, Incubus's Jose Pasillas, and Jon Theodore on the first Mars Volta album. Session ace Josh Freese is also here with his progressive band A Perfect Circle. And from the super-heavy side we feature the mind-boggling work of Danny Carey with Tool and Meshuggah's Tomas Haake. These players all push the envelope in the demanding world of prog.

Rush's
Neil Peart
Vapor Trails

MUSIC KEY

	Open	Half Open	R.C. Bell	C.C.
H.H.	O	∅	●	⊗
T.T.				
S.D.				
F.T.				
B.D.				
H.H. w/foot	X	B.D. 2	Add'l Toms	Ghost Note

The first Rush album of the twenty-first century exhibited a high-energy, modernized, radio-ready sound. Neil Peart's drumming seemed more groove-oriented than ever before. But, of course, Neil's fans got their money's worth, as *Vapor Trails* abounds with explosive drum fills and patterns. Here are a few examples.

"One Little Victory"

Neil fires the first salvo, as the album opens with this jarring double-kick train beat.

⊙ TRACK 120

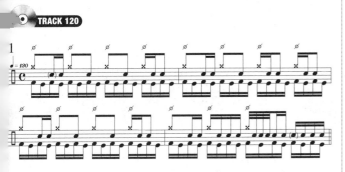

"Ghost Rider"

Even in a straightforward rock groove, Neil can always find a flourish to make the tune his own.

"How It Is"

Neil uses 16th-note hi-hat patterns throughout *Vapor Trails* to energize the songs. In the second verse of this tune, he mixes in a few syncopated crashes.

In the last chorus, Neil's signature ride cymbal playing brings the song to its climax.

"Vapor Trail"

The first verse of the title track features some wonderfully expressive hi-hat and snare drum work.

⊙ TRACK 121

This melodic tom-tom groove (beginning on a floor tom to the left of Neil's hi-hat) adds an earthy flow to the chorus, with a couple of splash cymbals thrown in for sweetening.

⊙ TRACK 122

"Nocturne"

An ebb-and-flow hi-hat part creates tension leading up to this song's final chorus. The tension-releasing fill is another Peart classic.

"Freeze"

It wouldn't be a Rush album without some odd time signatures. Here's Neil dancing around offbeats in a 5/4 section.

⊙ TRACK 123

Tool's
Danny Carey

Lateralus

Kevin Willis

Like each of their albums, the third release from prog metal masters Tool provided a spotlight for the prodigious talents of Danny Carey. The drumming on *Lateralus* had it all: imagination, dynamics, power, flash, and an unmistakably *human* feel. Danny cruised through Tool's odd time signatures with the mind of a mathematician. Let's check out a few examples.

"The Grudge"

This verse pattern divides itself into a 6/8-4/8 compound time signature. The hi-hat work spices it up.

"The Patient"

After a moody mid-song pause, Danny re-enters with this blazing double-bass sequence.

"Schism"

This beat locks note-for-note to a Justin Chancellor bass riff.

TRACK 124

The song ends with a ferocious double-bass pattern.

"Ticks & Leeches"

Tom-tom grooves abound on *Lateralus*. With the snares off in the intro of this tune, Danny creates a tribal effect, albeit a frantic one in 7/4 time!

TRACK 125

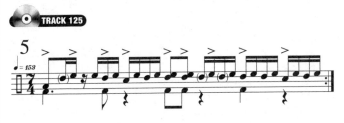

"Lateralus"

The title track features another compound time signature: a descending 9/8-8/8-7/8 cycle. Danny has the uncanny ability to make this kind of thing groove.

TRACK 126

"Reflection"

Here's another third world–sounding tom intro played with the snares off. (This one's in 4/4 time for a change!)

"Triad"

Finally, here's an amazing polyrhythmic pattern that builds to the climax of the song.

TRACK 127

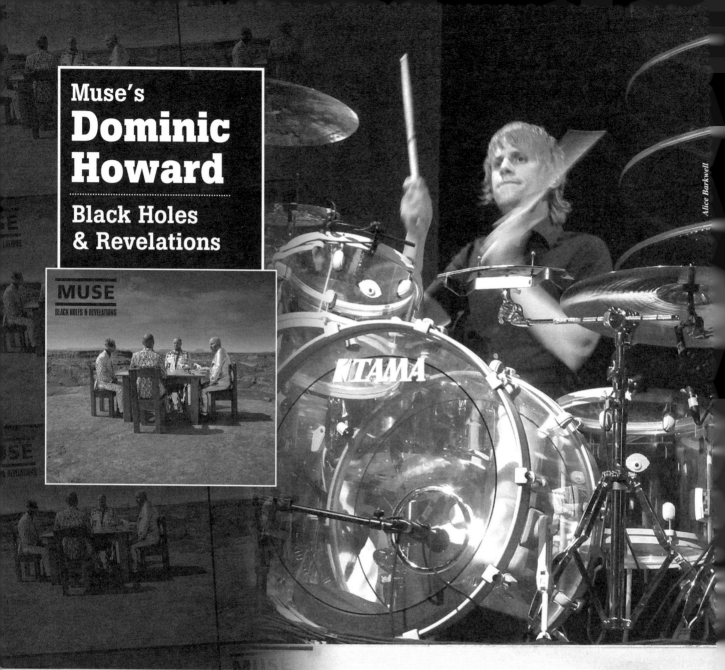

Muse's Dominic Howard

Black Holes & Revelations

Alice Barkwell

England's Muse soared into rock's upper echelon on the strength of their successful release *Black Holes & Revelations*. Buoyed by major airplay and touring, the band moved beyond early comparisons with Radiohead and Queen to forge their own musical identity. For his part, drummer Dominic Howard gave the band whatever it required, from delicate brush work to explosive prog-type fills. Though he can play simply when called upon, Howard has enough cool grooves and complicated riffs to warrant a closer look.

"Take A Bow"

The album's opening track is a scathing political indictment that builds to an explosive climax. When Dominic's groove enters, the slow 12/8 tempo allows the drummer to drop in 64th-note rolls and energetic snare/kick tradeoffs. (2:35)

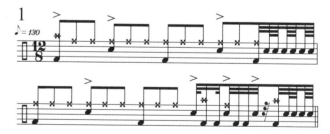

As the song nears its finish, Howard adds more bass drum and snare notes to his splashy ride beat, building intensity right to the end. (3:35)

"Map Of The Problematique"

A tom beat dominates the first half of this dance-groove track before Dominic changes to a 16th-note hi-hat pattern for the remainder of the song. The connecting section between the two grooves is this aggressive snare and crash pattern that jumps right out of the speakers. This part also doubles as a perfect ending for the song. (2:10)

"Invincible"

After setting the tone with a marching snare pattern early in this tune, Howard adds a U2-like feel to the track with this 16th-note hi-hat beat featuring displaced snare and tom accents. (2:32)

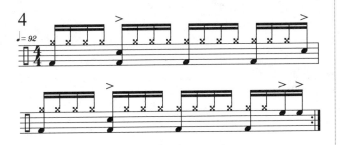

The song's instrumental section begins with this 16th-note sequence, played in unison by the band until Dominic's triplet fill releases into the guitar/synth solo. (3:45)

"Assassin"

Muse's occasional prog leanings are on display in the intro of this track. Howard locks to the band's fast 16th-note riff with his drum pattern, embellishing it with some 32nd-note snare work before ending in a flashy triplet fill. (0:24)

TRACK 128

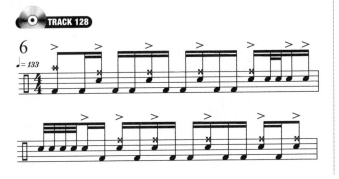

The song ends on the same instrumental sequence, where Dominic drops in another quick fill punctuated by two accents on a China cymbal. These over-the-bar fills show off the drummer's adventurous and sophisticated style. (3:18)

TRACK 129

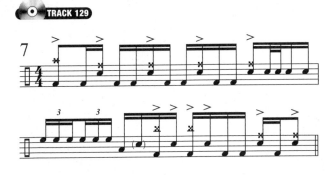

"City Of Delusion"

This verse beat matches up to the tune's syncopated guitar rhythms, which is held together by a steady quarter-note bell pattern. (0:43)

Dominic enhances the Middle Eastern flavor of the track with this wonderful groove in the second part of the verse. The hand drum–inspired fill included here adds to the effect. (1:01)

TRACK 130

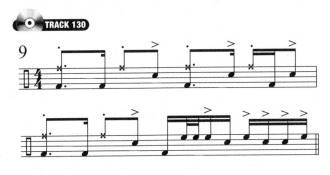

"Knights Of Cydonia"

The album's closer races along on Howard's galloping offbeat hi-hat groove. It's the perfect groove to express the imagery of the song's title. (0:50)

Jon Theodore

The Mars Volta's
De-Loused In The Comatorium

The debut album from The Mars Volta took prog rock in new directions with high-energy odd time signatures and unusual sonic textures. The band's indefinable blend of punk, jazz-fusion, metal, and Middle Eastern rhythms formed a fertile soundscape for drummer Jon Theodore to explore. And explore he did, with some wonderfully quirky and creative patterns. Here are a few examples.

"Son Et Lumiere"

Jon's entrance on the album comes near the end of this short atmospheric intro piece, and makes an immediate explosive statement.

"Inertiatic ESP"

One of rock music's most underused time signatures is 3/4, a situation rectified by The Mars Volta on this album. A four-note guitar riff over the following three-beat groove adds a compelling polyrhythm to the verse of this track.

"Roulette Dares (The Haunt Of)"

In this song, Jon creates a cool effect by making his cymbal pattern part of the movement of his drumbeat, rather than just a simple steady timekeeping device.

"Drunkship Of Lanterns"

The bridge of this tune contains two different drum patterns based around a staccato guitar riff. Jon mimics the staccato effect in the first figure, then turns it into a flowing groove in the second.

"Eriatarka"

Here's another unusual drumbeat with a moving cymbal pattern. The excitement in Jon's grooves stems from his unique rhythmic approach to high-speed drumming.

TRACK 131

"Cicatriz ESP"

In this two-handed, 16th-note hi-hat beat from the verse of the tune, the bass and snare combination doubles a syncopated bass guitar riff.

Jon's chorus pattern contains some syncopation of its own.

TRACK 132

"This Apparatus Must Be Unearthed"

This intro pattern features a nice contrast between a fast tom lick in the first measure and an off-beat open hi-hat sequence in the second.

TRACK 133

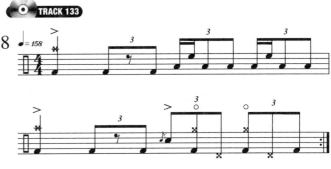

Meshuggah's
Tomas Haake
obZen

Of all the approaches to odd-time drumming, Tomas Haake's work with math-metal wizards Meshuggah is one of the most fascinating and difficult to grasp. Instead of simply designing odd-time beats to match odd-time riffs, or playing straightforward 4/4 beats under complex time changes, Haake pulls off both at the same time. To understand what he's doing, let's take a look at some of his grooves from Meshuggah's *obZen* album.

"Electric Red"

Our first example is from the outtro of this track. Bass and guitars are playing a syncopated riff in 9/8, which Haake matches note-for-note with his kick drum. He's playing quarter notes (with occasional extra accents) on his crash, which causes the cymbal pattern to switch between downbeats and offbeats from measure to measure. Tomas also plants a snare hit on every fourth cymbal note. This causes the snare to move forward one beat in each successive measure. The result is a repeating eight-measure cycle. (5:01)

🔘 **TRACK 134**

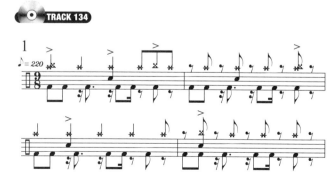

You can also look at the previous pattern in 4/4. Example 2 is the same section as in Example 1, only written in 4/4 instead of 9/8. It takes nine measures of 4/4 to match the eight measures of 9/8.

In 4/4, the cymbal and snare play on the downbeats, while the syncopated kick pattern is delayed one 8th note in each measure in order to match up with the nine-beat guitar riff. As a result, Haake is playing in two time signatures at once—his hands are in 4/4, while his feet are in 9/8.

"Lethargica"

The verse of this track contains a nineteen-beat guitar/bass riff. Once again, Tomas matches his kick pattern to the riff while playing in 4/4 with his hands. To make it easier to follow, we've divided the nineteen-beat pattern into groupings of 7/8, 5/8, and 7/8. This phrase takes six measures (twice through the nineteen-beat riff) for the cymbal to return to downbeats at the start of the pattern. The snare takes many more measures to return to its original position. (0:36)

Here's the same sequence (with a couple of extra notes) written in 4/4. Notice how difficult it is to pick out the repeating kick pattern when it's written this way. (The pattern starts over every nineteen 8th notes). The arrows indicate where the bass drum pattern repeats.

"Bleed"

Here's another intricate polyrhythm, this time featuring flashy double bass work. The pattern is a cluster of two 32nd notes and two 16th notes, which takes up the space of three 16th notes. Haake opens this song by repeating this riff on his double kicks against a half-time hand pattern. It takes three measures for the pattern to complete its cycle. (0:00)

TRACK 135

"obZen"

This track features a seventeen-beat repeating riff, which Tomas again mirrors on his kick drums under a 4/4 snare and cymbal pattern. In the sixteen-bar sequence in Example 6, notice how the bass drum pattern repeats one beat later in each four-bar phrase. (0:00)

"Pravus"

Here's an example of Tomas using a more conventional approach to odd-time playing. This tune opens with a twenty-three-note guitar riff, which we've divided into 5/8, 6/8, and 7/8. Haake picks up the accents in the riff with snare/crashes as he drives the groove with his double kick pattern. Though not as complex as the previous examples, the changing accents in this groove make the track sound very compelling. (0:00)

TRACK 136

A Perfect Circle's
Josh Freese
Thirteenth Step

Alex Solca

MUSIC KEY

The second album from modern art rockers A Perfect Circle was titled *Thirteenth Step*. With Tool frontman Maynard Keenan's distinctive vocal style setting the mood, comparisons between the drumming of Josh Freese and Tool's Danny Carey were inevitable. Josh's patterns, while not as complicated as math-rock mastermind Carey's, are consistently interesting and creative, and completely suit the band's dreamy compositions. Freese also brings rare taste and feel to his playing, with just enough flash to keep things exciting.

"The Package"

Josh's double bass lick adds explosiveness to the end of the lead track's bridge (at the 4:41 mark of the tune).

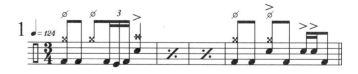

"Weak And Powerless"

A repetitive staccato 6/8 beat relentlessly drives the verse of this song. Note the subtle difference between the last beat of each measure. (0:23)

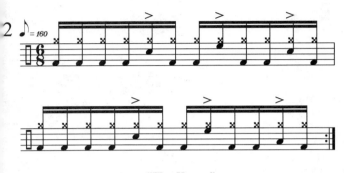

"The Noose"

The re-intro drum beat in this song features great accent and drag work, coupled with an unusual stop/start effect. The result spells *groove* with a capital G! (1:52)

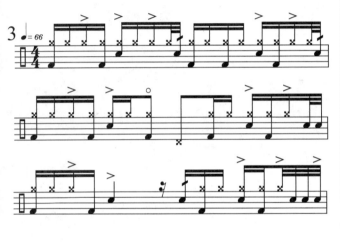

"Blue"

Josh gives a rhythmic twist to the drum fill leading into the first chorus of this tune. (1:08)

"Vanishing"

Here's a wonderful idea for a cymbal part. The two-handed alternating ride cymbal and hi-hat pattern sounds like a strange echo in this half-time verse groove. (1:11)

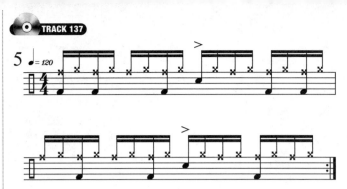

"The Outsider"

This little gem of a beat immediately follows the song's first chorus. Notice the two-against-three polyrhythm of the bass drum pattern in this 6/8 groove. (1:17)

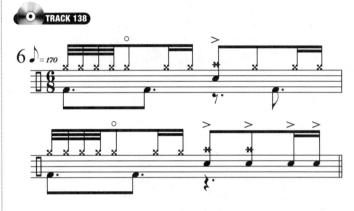

"Crimes"

Here's one of those drum beats that sounds like it's in an odd time signature but is really in 4/4. Freese accomplishes this with the displacement of his tom and bass drum, coupled with the movement of the snare backbeat. (0:58)

"Gravity"

On the other hand, Josh's 7/8 groove makes this song feel as smooth and comfortable as it would if he were playing in 4/4 time. (0:24)

Yes's
Bill Bruford
Fragile

Bill Bruford is the dean of progressive drummers. His work over the past forty years with Yes, King Crimson, Earthworks, and many other projects has earned him the admiration of rock and jazz musicians alike. Yes's breakout fourth album, *Fragile,* was a head-turning introduction to Bruford's ringing rimshot snare, complex rhythmic patterns, and rudimental mastery. Here are some examples from this prog classic.

"Roundabout"

This hit single jumped out of the radio speakers in 1972, courtesy of Chris Squire's catchy bass line and Bruford's rimshot backbeat. The chorus is a showcase for Bruford's signature snare sound, as he pounds out a broken quarter–note pattern over Rick Wakeman's organ riffs. (2:50)

As the song moves towards its climax, this fill leads out of Steve Howe's guitar solo. Bill's kick drum notes elevate the fill's excitement level. (6:27)

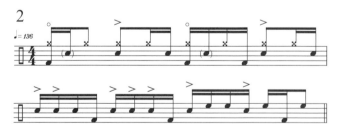

"South Side Of The Sky"

The opening fill from this track demonstrates a pattern that Bruford uses in various spots on the album: a triplet move between the hands and bass drum with a RL-LR sticking. (0:17)

This song contains a lengthy middle section where Bill takes a free-flowing improvisational approach. The odd time signature and Bruford's jazzy snare work create a stark contrast to the song's opening and closing hard-edged rock sections. (3:25)

"Five Percent For Nothing"

Bruford's quirky composition for the album is built around this beat based on the right-left-kick sticking pattern, this time in 16th notes between the hi-hat, snare, and bass drum. (0:00)

TRACK 141

"Long Distance Runaround"

Here's the second big hit from *Fragile*, with another beat displaying Bruford's unique brand of controlled randomness. No straight backbeat here. (0:12)

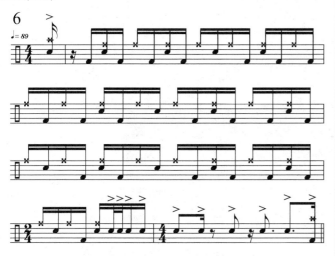

"The Fish (Schindleria Praematurus)"

Chris Squire's solo composition for layered bass guitars benefits from Bill's effortless odd-time drumming. This time it's 7/8, and his broken quarter-note snare pattern drives the music here much as it does in the chorus of "Roundabout." (0:08)

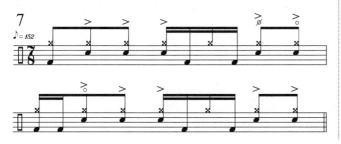

"Heart Of The Sunrise"

This long piece contains great examples of Bruford's use of rudimental sticking patterns. The basic beat (as shown in the first two measures) combines a RLRRLL paradiddle-diddle with single strokes. The fill leading out of this groove employs syncopation, accent control, and shifting rhythms—all Bruford specialties. (0:18)

TRACK 142

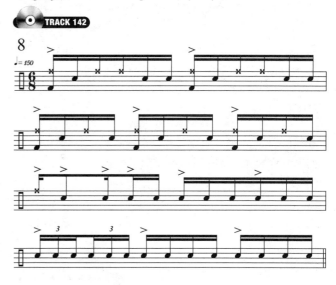

After the intensity of the opening groove, the song breaks down to a slower, funkier section. It starts with a classic misdirected beginning, as Bill displaces his snare and kick drum for the first two measures, before returning to a more-or-less normal groove in measure 3. Notice the cool stick work in the triplet fills. (0:32)

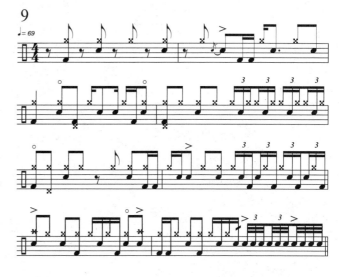

A short, fast 5/8 section later in the tune gives Bruford an opportunity to revisit his paradiddle-diddle sticking pattern in a different rhythm. (6:52)

TRACK 143

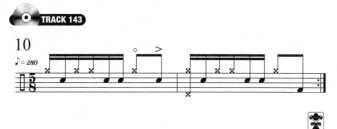

Incubus's
Jose Pasillas
Morning View

Brian Smith

Incubus followed up their multi-platinum breakthrough album, *Make Yourself*, by expanding into more progressive territories. *Morning View* provided a wealth of sonic delights, one of which is the drumming of Jose Pasillas. As usual, Jose's popping snare drove the music along, while he energized the band with his intricate drum patterns. Let's look at a few examples.

"Nice To Know You"

This up-tempo verse groove takes a disorienting turn when Jose follows a measure of 2/4 with an off-beat snare accent in the next measure.

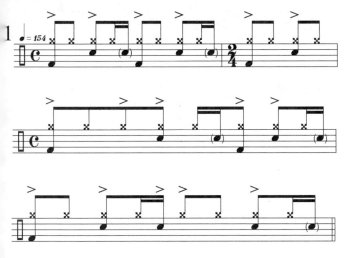

"Wish You Were Here"

Jose spices up his playing with subtle details, like occasional 16th and 32nd notes on the hi-hat in the second verse of this tune.

TRACK 144

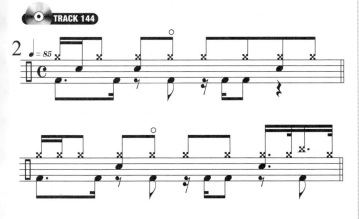

"Blood On The Ground"

Here's a terrifically quirky fill from this song's bridge. Jose utilizes the whole drumkit while hardly ever hitting the same piece twice in a row.

TRACK 145

"Warning"

The ending of this track features some extraordinary cymbal work.

TRACK 146

"Echo"

Jose uses brush-sticks on this tune for a delicate change of pace.

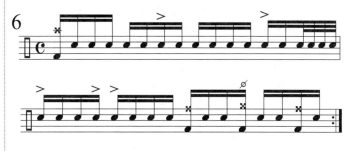

Brush-sticks are also perfect for fast single and double strokes on the snare drum, as in this pre-chorus pattern.

"Have You Ever"

Jose's use of high-pitched tom flourishes in his beats brings to mind the Police-era drumming of Stewart Copeland.

"Are You In?"

The album's funkiest tune opens with this around-the-toms-and-back triplet fill. Movement around the drumset with triplets is easier to pull off using the following sticking patterns: RRL and/or RLL.

Genesis's
Phil Collins
The Prog-Rock Years

MUSIC KEY

		splash
	R.C. Bell	✳
open H.H.	○	
T.T.		
S.D.		
F.T.		
B.D.		
H.H. w/ foot		Add'l T.T.

After two and a half decades as a major pop star, it's easy to forget that Phil Collins began his rock career as one of England's premiere drummers. But Collins' years with Genesis contain some of early prog rock's most technically amazing and creatively inspiring drumming.

Collins came into Genesis in the early '70s, after the band had shifted through several drummers on their first two albums. Influenced by American jazz and R&B drummers, Collins' presence—along with the arrival of guitarist Steve Hackett—energized the band, triggering a long run of critically and commercially successful albums. Here's a look back at the work of one of Britain's best.

Foxtrot (1972)
"Watcher Of The Skies"

By his second album with Genesis, Phil proved to be a perfect match for the music's intricate rhythms. Here he plays a unison snare/cymbal pattern over a quarter-note kick pulse. (2:30)

1

"Supper's Ready (Apocalypse In 9/8)"

One of Collins' most important contributions to the band was his ability to make odd time signatures groove. His earthy feel helped keep things from sounding too grandiose. A great example is in his playing on the "Apocalypse In 9/8" section of this multi-part composition. His syncopated playing is a highlight, but never keeps the section from driving forward. Notice the quick Bonham-like footwork in the fourth measure. (17:03)

TRACK 147

2

Selling England By The Pound (1973)
"The Battle Of Epping Forest"

Selling England By The Pound is considered by some fans to be Genesis's best album. Throughout this record, Phil's handling of odd times seems effortless. The syncopation in this 7/4 groove helps to disguise its odd meter. (1:50)

3

"The Cinema Show"

Contrast the semi-relaxed feel of the previous 7/4 beat with this high-energy 7/8 pattern. Collins' open hi-hat work is crucial to the feel of the groove. (6:00)

TRACK 148

4

The Lamb Lies Down On Broadway (1974)
"Back In N.Y.C."

On Peter Gabriel's last album with Genesis, Phil Collins is in top form. This track features a different take on 7/8, with Phil establishing a half-time effect in his groove. (1:18)

"The Colony Of Slippermen (The Raven)"

Here's a cool fill that breaks up two grooves from the fast 12/8 section of this track. This is a good example of Collins' incredible use of ghost notes. (5:36)

A Trick Of The Tail (1976)
"Dance On A Volcano"

If fans thought Peter Gabriel's departure would spell the end of Genesis, they were stunned when the band delivered one of their finest albums—with Phil Collins as the frontman. Though touring called for an additional drummer (Bill Bruford, then Chester Thompson), Collins still drummed on the records. Here he demonstrates another creative slant on the band's favorite time signature. (3:00)

TRACK 149

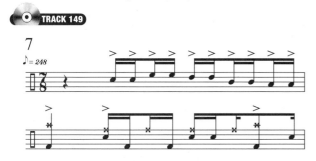

"Robbery, Assault And Battery"

This track contains a tricky alternating 7/8 and 6/8 pattern. Collins handles the phrase by ending the 6/8 measures with a four-beat fill, which helps emphasize the downbeat of each thirteen-beat sequence. His accent work adds to the rhythmic flow. (3:18)

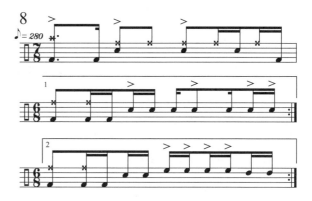

Wind & Wuthering (1976)
"All In A Mouse's Night"

Guitarist Steve Hackett's final album with Genesis also signaled the end of the band's prog-rock sound. From here, Phil Collins' pop sensibility began to take over, which caused his drumming to become a little more spacious. After a sweeping fill in this track, Phil mixes a frantic pattern in the first few beats of the measure with an open feel in the second half. (3:18)

"...In That Quiet Earth"

Despite Collins' shift towards a less cluttered playing style, he could still come up with a slick 9/8 groove when the song demanded. This one has the hi-hat and ride blasting away in unison. (0:06)

And Then There Were Three (1978)
"Down And Out"

Now down to just Phil Collins, keyboardist Tony Banks, and bassist/guitarist Mike Rutherford, Genesis underwent a transition for their next album, which contains progressive tunes, ballads, and the pop single "Follow You Follow Me." From here on, Genesis became a radio-friendly hit-maker. Still, Collins exposes his fusion roots at times, like in this fill and groove from the lead track. (0:43)

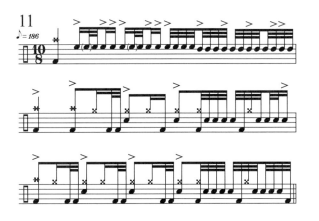

"The Lady Lies"

In this song, Phil plays paradiddles between the snare and cymbal bell during the chorus. (0:59)

Duke (1980)
"Duke's Travels"

Duke's pop-oriented production spawned two hit singles and broke Genesis to a much wider audience in the US. The band returns to its prog roots at the end of the album with this extended piece. Here's a moment from the middle of the track where Collins drops a triplet rhythm into his quarter-note snare groove. (5:14)

"Duke's End"

Collins' short solo break in the album's closing instrumental reminds you that he's still a hot-shot drummer. Check out his quick bass drum foot. (0:42)

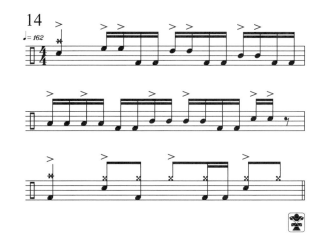

Chapter 6

Classic Rock Greats

Our last chapter puts the focus on an earlier genera-tion of drummers whose work influenced many of the younger players in this book. Included are some of the greatest names in rock drumming history. From the '60s we look at Ringo Starr's beloved work with The Beatles, Keith Moon's drumming madness with The Who, and Mitch Mitchell's elegant playing with The Jimi Hendrix Experience.

Moving to the '70s, we examine the work of two giants: Led Zeppelin's John Bonham and Levon Helm from The Band. From later in that decade comes the standout drumming of Van Halen's Alex Van Halen and Stewart Copeland with The Police.

Several decades are spanned in our special look at the impressive career of Cozy Powell and the impeccable drummers of Steely Dan. Each player featured in this chapter displayed a unique voice on the instrument that helped bring rock drumming to where it is today.

The Jimi Hendrix Experience's
Mitch Mitchell

Axis: Bold As Love

Tom Copi

MUSIC KEY

open	O	C.C. ✳
H.H.	R.C. ✕	
T.T.		
S.D.		
F.T.		
B.D.		
H.H. w/ foot	ghost-note	

Jimi Hendrix is arguably the greatest of all rock guitarists. His band featured drummer Mitch Mitchell, who himself took a back seat to no one on his instrument in the late '60s. The musical relationship between Hendrix and Mitchell was profound, each pushing the other to new heights of improvisational brilliance. This month we take a look back at a key recording that captured one of the finest drummers of that unforgettable era.

Hendrix released two albums in 1967, his debut, *Are You Experienced*, and the follow-up, *Axis: Bold As Love*. While the first album contains classic hits like "Purple Haze" and "Foxey Lady," *Axis* is sonically more experimental and stylistically diverse, which is reflected in Mitchell's creative drum parts. Here are some examples.

"Up From The Skies"

Axis opens with Hendrix imitating a spaceship launch using nothing but guitar feedback effects. Then the album takes an unexpected turn into this jazz-tinged track, which displays Mitch Mitchell's finesse on a swirling brush groove. Example 1 is his famous intro fill for this song. Notice how the last note of each triplet moves down the tones of the kit. (0:00)

"Spanish Castle Magic"

The album finally moves in a rock direction on its third track. Mitchell mirrors Jimi's guitar rhythms for the song's verses, slightly swinging the 16th notes in his pattern. For the chorus, his beat works closely with Hendrix's vocal phrasing. The delayed snare hit on the "&" of beat 4 (measures 5 and 6) provides an interesting push/pull effect to his splashy crash/ride chorus groove. This sequence shows the end of the first verse into the chorus pattern. (0:23)

"Wait Until Tomorrow"

This tune contains some of Hendrix's finest rhythm-guitar work, along with several memorable fills from Mitchell. Here's the end of the first chorus, where Mitch's two-bar break (measures 3 and 4) brings the energy down into the guitar-only re-intro. (0:37)

TRACK 150

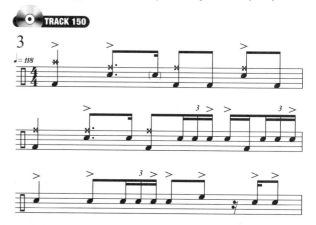

"Little Wing"

This is one of Hendrix's most-loved ballads. After Jimi's breathtaking guitar intro, Mitchell's entrance fill is a true classic, as important to the track as the guitar work. (0:32)

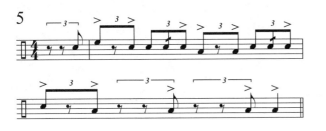

The fill leading into the second verse is just as powerful. Mitchell's strategically placed double strokes create a wonderful sliding effect. (1:04)

"If 6 Was 9"

Mitchell's hi-hat pattern for the intro and verses of this tune remains as one of rock's most recognizable drum parts. His jazz influences take over in the chorus as he leads through the chord changes with an improvisational approach, blurring the lines between beats and fills. (0:34)

"Castles Made Of Sand"

Though remembered as a chops-heavy player, Mitchell was also very tasteful and musical. In the verses of this song, his pattern is straightforward (measure 1). Then during the non-vocal interlude between verses, Mitch pulls out a cool 16th-note snare pattern (measures 3 and 4) to keep the interest up for the two-bar sequence. (0:24)

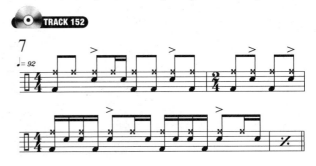

"She's So Fine"

On this song by Experience bassist Noel Redding, Mitchell comes up with another memorable beat. A few years later, Keith Moon would use a similar concept—placing a recurring fill inside of a beat—for several Who tunes, though his patterns usually featured a triplet ruff. Mitchell's is in straight 16ths. (0:11)

"Little Miss Lover"

Hendrix lets Mitch's strong funk beat start this track for several measures. The two offbeat snare hits are slightly delayed to enhance the depth of the groove. (0:00)

"Bold As Love"

Mitchell reuses his chorus beat from "Spanish Castle Magic" on the choruses of the album's closer. However, this time the tempo is slower, and the feel is swung. It's another example of Mitch bringing his jazzy approach to Hendrix's bluesy rock style, a magical combination that sounds as compelling today as it did forty years ago. (0:29)

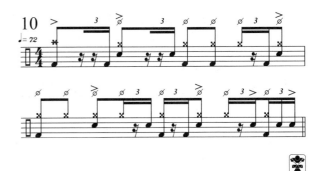

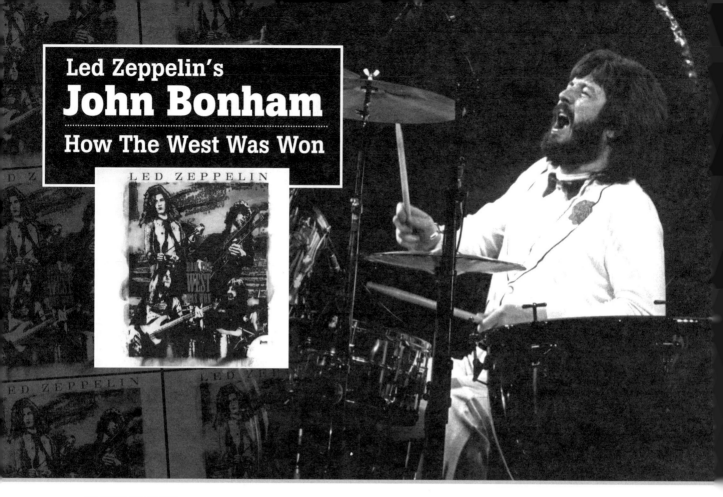

Led Zeppelin's
John Bonham
How The West Was Won

MUSIC KEY

This three-CD live set from Led Zeppelin is one of the most important "lost tape" discoveries of all time, documenting an incredible performance by a beloved band at the absolute height of its powers. All four members shine here, but John Bonham is especially impressive, with his powerful drumming mixed right out front. You can feel the impact of his attack as he improvises on his well-known drum parts, playing off of Jimmy Page's guitar riffs.

"Immigrant Song"

The first drum fill on the album comes early in the opening verse of this track, and lets you know that you're in for a great Bonham performance.

TRACK 153

In the song's bridge, Bonham switches to a splashy ride cymbal groove, playing around with his normal pattern in the second and third measure of this sequence.

TRACK 154

"Heartbreaker"

The album abounds with classic Bonham-isms, sometimes in unexpected places. The following fill is similar to the famous one from the guitar solo in "Whole Lotta Love," only here it leads into the second verse of this Zeppelin favorite.

"Black Dog"

An often overlooked aspect of John Bonham's drumming is his sensitivity to the playing of Jimmy Page and John Paul Jones. This unusual groove, from the first bridge of the tune, locks completely to Page's guitar riff.

Here's another famous Bonham lick, a 16th-note-triplet bass drum flourish, this time landing in the song's guitar solo section.

TRACK 155

"Since I've Been Loving You"

Bonham could play a slow 12/8 blues like no one else. Check out the syncopation in this fill from early in the song. His ever-present left-foot hi-hat would pop up to keep him on track in rambling fills like this one.

TRACK 156

"Stairway To Heaven"

Zeppelin's most famous song contains some inspired drumming as well. This fill, which leads into the ending guitar solo, is simply explosive.

Check out the way Bonham turns the beat around just before the song's final verse.

"Dazed And Confused"

Bonham had an uncanny knack for negotiating his way around syncopated fills in a 12/8 blues feel. Take this sequence, for example, from his entrance in this early Zeppelin gem. (This kicks in at the 1:53 point of the track.)

TRACK 157

"The Crunge"

During the extended-jam middle section of "Dazed And Confused" (at the 15:37 mark), the band slips into this song, an odd James Brown tribute that contains one of Bonham's most unusual grooves.

TRACK 158

"Moby Dick"

John Bonham's legendary solo sees perhaps its greatest rendition on this album, clocking in at almost twenty minutes of pure drumming bliss. Bonham moves gracefully and powerfully through his repertoire, at times playing barehanded, with a tambourine affixed to his hi-hat keeping time. Here's a smattering of different licks from the solo. (Check out how fast he's playing these patterns!)

"Whole Lotta Love"

Here's another example of a memorable chorus pattern (beginning at the 1:22 mark) that receives a more fully realized treatment in this live performance.

This fill from the third verse (at the 4:27 point of the song) blends back into the groove via some offbeat crash work.

Bonham's long fill leading into the song's ending (at the 21:05 mark) takes a syncopated turn in the second measure. This move is easier to play if the ghost notes on the snare are double-stroked.

 TRACK 159

"Rock And Roll"

Finally, here's the famous solo ending to this song, extended by Bonham in this live performance. Bonzo's climatic repeating 16th-note pattern starts here as a five-note grouping, then quickly blends into four notes, and of course continues much longer than on the original studio version.

Cozy Powell

A Retrospective In Rock

On the all-time list of important British rock drummers, one name that often goes unfairly overlooked is Cozy Powell. Unlike John Bonham (Led Zeppelin), Keith Moon (The Who), Ginger Baker (Cream), or Ian Paice (Deep Purple), Powell isn't linked to one hugely successful act. Cozy was a rock 'n' roll nomad, moving from band to band every few years while amassing a long list of credits. Through it all, Powell's dynamic playing left a giant influence on the hard rock and metal drummers of his era.

Jeff Beck, Jeff Beck Group (1972)
"Ice Cream Cakes"

After starting his career as a session player in England, Powell first attained international acclaim as a member of the early-'70s Jeff Beck Group. Beck showcased Cozy by having him open this album with the following interesting intro. The toms-to-bass triplet ruff would become a favorite Powell lick. (0:00)

TRACK 160

"Going Down"

Beck turned this blues tune into a high-energy funk classic. Cozy opened his one-handed 16th notes on the backbeat to help deepen the groove. Here's the end of the second chorus, where Powell switches to a paradiddle kick/snare groove under driving 8th notes on the bell of the ride. (1:55)

Rainbow, Rising (1976) "Starstruck"

When Jeff Beck dissolved his group to make way for Beck Bogert & Appice (with Carmine Appice on drums), Cozy went back to doing sessions, including a few releases under his own name. In 1976, he began one of his longer stretches as a bandmember when he joined Ritchie Blackmore's Rainbow.

Rising, their first recording together, became a seminal album in the development of heavy metal. This is where Powell's reputation as a double bass powerhouse begins to take hold. While many rock drummers at this time were using double kicks primarily in solos and end-of-song rave-ups, Powell began working them into fills and grooves wherever he could. Here's an example from the end of the first verse in "Starstruck." (0:49)

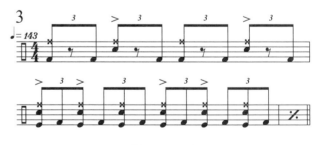

"Stargazer"

This cut, the musical heart of the album, is an eight-minute metal opus containing some outstanding drumming. Powell opens the song with a short solo that's based around another one of his signature riffs: the right-left-bass-bass quad. The fact that Blackmore let Cozy take the intro to this key song indicates how important his drumming was to the sound of the band. (0:00)

Cozy's quad lick returns during the chorus. (1:23)

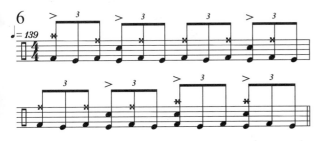

Black Sabbath, Headless Cross (1989)
"Devil & Daughter"

After five years with Rainbow, Powell decided it was time for a change. He worked both with Michael Schenker and Whitesnake for a time, along with the short-lived Emerson, Lake & Powell, before winding up in Black Sabbath in the late '80s. Cozy co-produced *Headless Cross*, and his drumming is mixed up front and drenched in the era's huge gated-reverb sound. Here's his triplet double bass groove from the guitar solo section of "Devil & Daughter." (2:53)

"Call Of The Wild"

In the out-chorus of this song, Powell executes another classic fill. This one clusters quads into twelve-note groupings so that he can return to his snare accent on the fourth beat of the measure. (4:49)

"Rightwing"

The fade-out of the album's last track features some great riffing over double-kick 16th notes. Here, Cozy works an against-the-beat phrase with snare, toms, and crash cymbals. (6:15)

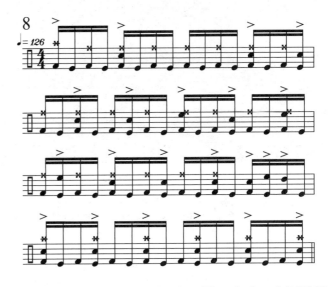

Yngwie Malmsteen, Facing The Animal (1998)
"Enemy"

Powell was in and out of Sabbath over the next several years, and continued with other projects until he landed with Yngwie Malmsteen in 1997. Many years of recording had honed Cozy's playing into a lean blend of power and groove, which was the right approach to accompany the Swedish guitar hero. Here's his cool 7/8 beat from an Yngwie composition with prog-rock overtones. (0:22)

"Poison In Your Veins"

Near the end of the album, Cozy pulled out his favorite quad lick for a blazing fill at the climax of this song. (3:26)

Three months after the release of *Facing The Animal*, Cozy Powell was on a break from touring with Malmsteen when he crashed his car. Cozy's injuries proved fatal, bringing to a close the long and varied career of one of England's finest hard rock drummers.

The Who's
Keith Moon
His Craziest Licks

What if you were asked by The Who to fill the drum chair long vacated by one of the most unique drummers in rock music history? If you're Zak Starkey, you simply take the ideas you learned from Keith Moon when you were a boy, combine them with your own outstanding technique and control (along with your love of The Who and Moon's drumming), and you're good to go. For the rest of us, here's a smattering of Keith's coolest licks, in case we ever get the call.

The Who Sing My Generation (1965)
"Anyway, Anyhow, Anywhere"

With its wild extended instrumental bridge, this single was an early example of the "Manic Moon" approach to drumming. Keith flashes his Gene Krupa influence in this floor tom groove from the song's ending sequence. (2:24)

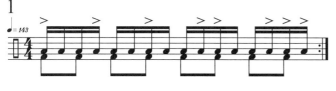

"Substitute" (1966)

By the time The Who recorded this hit single (available on the *30 Years Of Maximum R&B* box set), the improvisational nature of Moon's playing was fully developed. Here he twists the beat around, playing off of Pete Townshend's guitar rhythms in the song's final re-intro. Even at this early point in his career, Moon's signature 8th-note bass drum adds that familiar feeling of excitement to every drum break. (2:30)

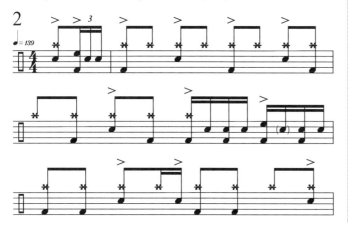

The Who Sell Out (1967)
"I Can See For Miles"

The popular view is that Moon's drumming consisted mostly of cymbal bashing and flurries of reckless tom fills. But Keith's flair for the dramatic could occasionally lead him in more controlled, composed directions. The powerful opening of this classic Who single was achieved by double-tracking the drums. In one channel, Moon lays a bed of continuous 8th notes on the ride and bass drum, splashing the cymbal on chord changes. (0:00)

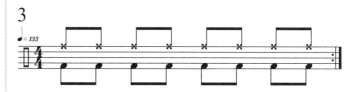

In the other channel, Keith takes an almost orchestral approach, overdubbing tom and snare accents and crescendos to create a menacing mood for the intro. (0:00)

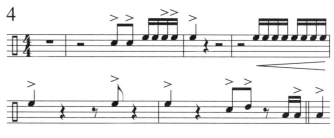

Tommy (1969) "Pinball Wizard"

This lick from the end of the bridge in "Pinball Wizard" perfectly encapsulates the appeal of Moon's layered approach to drum fills. He creates a quick crescendo (the gradually opening hi-hat) and decrescendo (the fall-down-the-stairs triplet ruff) while dropping offbeat snare accents over his bass drum pulse. (1:36)

Live At Leeds (1970) "Happy Jack"

Here's the complete drum part for the first chorus of "Happy Jack" from one of rock's greatest live albums. Moon's explosive fills are made all the more impressive by their contrast to the song's sparse verse. (0:37)

Who's Next (1971) "Won't Get Fooled Again"

No look at Moon's drumming would be complete without his short solo at the end of the synthesizer breakdown in this classic track. Keith works a syncopated theme over his ubiquitous 8th-note kick drum pattern that builds in intensity before launching into a long 16th-note snare roll that explodes into Roger Daltrey's scream. This is one of rock's defining moments. (7:31)

Quadrophenia (1973) "The Punk And The Godfather"

Moon's accents play a dual role in this 16th note–triplet fill. They preserve the pulse of the pattern, while also creating an ebb and flow to his sweep around the kit. The last beat of the fill contains another Moonism. Here he separates his hands between different drums during a roll to create a fuller sound. (1:38)

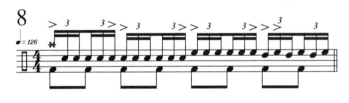

Who Are You (1978) "Who Are You"

Keith managed to squeeze some cool licks into his last album with The Who, despite the toll that his extreme lifestyle had begun to take on his playing. Moon's fills and 16th-note bass drums keep the energy going during the half-time verses of this title track. (5:02)

Van Halen's
Alex Van Halen
The Early Years

MUSIC KEY

open
H.H.   R.C.   C.C.
T.T.
S.D.
F.T.
B.D.1
H.H.   B.D.2   Add I
w/ foot   T.T.

Though guitar god Eddie Van Halen's groundbreaking techniques have brought him more fame through the years, musicians and fans alike know that Alex Van Halen is a top-notch player in his own right. Let's examine his best moments on some of Van Halen's biggest David Lee Roth–era songs.

Van Halen (1978)
"Runnin' With The Devil"

This hit from Van Halen's first album has all the band's trademarks in place: Roth's signature screams, a great guitar riff from Eddie, and Alex's bedrock beat. Notice his semi-open hi-hat accents on the backbeats, which add depth to the groove. (0:29)

At the end of the song Alex accents every beat, first with a floor tom/snare drum tradeoff separated by ride-cymbal offbeats, and then with grabbed crashes. (3:23)

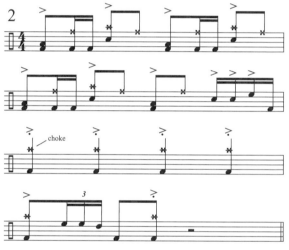

"You Really Got Me"

In the chorus of Van Halen's cover of this Kinks classic, Alex seems to be paying tribute to a drummer from another celebrated British band. This crash cymbal–heavy beat and triplet ruff was one of Who drummer Keith Moon's staple moves. (1:15)

Van Halen II (1979)
"Dance The Night Away"

The pre-chorus of this single from the second Van Halen album is built on dramatic accents from the band. After simply stating the accents in the first bar, Alex sets up the accents with fills in the remaining measures. (1:25)

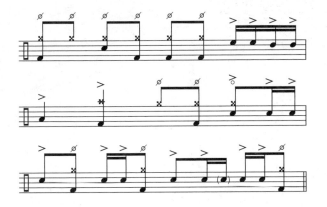

"Beautiful Girls"

Built around another compelling guitar riff from Eddie, this track swings hard in a half-time feel. Alex uses the traditional jazz ride pattern while catching offbeat accents in the pre-chorus groove. (0:38)

TRACK 166

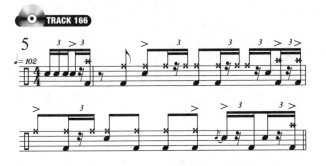

Fair Warning (1982)
"Unchained"

Alex handles the odd-time section of this track by locking in with Eddie's guitar riff as he negotiates the changing time signatures. The end of the sequence features more of Alex's favorite grabbed crashes. (0:42)

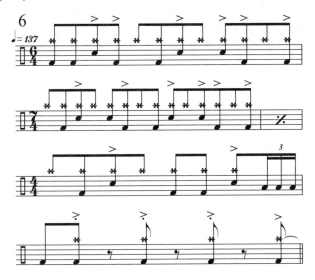

MCMLXXXIV (1984) "Jump"

This massive hit features another interesting pre-chorus sequence, with Alex alternating between the ride, hi-hat, and snare in a repeating three-note pattern. (0:57)

"Hot For Teacher"

Now we come to Alex's best-known beat. His incredible performance on this track ranks up with the best drumming of the era. In his opening solo sequence, Alex layers a triplet pattern on a deep tom (or low-pitched Simmons pad) over a classic double bass shuffle. (0:06)

TRACK 167

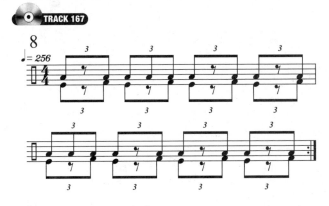

When Alex launches into the main groove, he plays double strokes on the ride cymbal to fill in every other triplet over the double kick shuffle. Check the tempo of these grooves—he's flying! (0:23)

TRACK 168

Alex brings the band out of the song's breakdown sections with some quick, flashy licks. This one is from the second breakdown. (2:14)

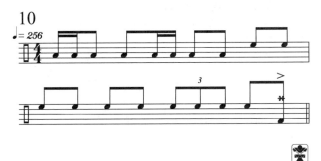

The Band's
Levon Helm
His Greatest Grooves

Levon Helm is the quintessential American drummer. Combining a musical upbringing in the melting pot of the Mid-South with years of dues-paying road work, Levon's playing distills the country's major indigenous music styles—blues, country, jazz, and rock 'n' roll.

Levon also mixes in deep musical sensitivity that he developed as a soulful vocalist. All of this gives him a unique perspective that few drummers share. Though most often appreciated as a "feel" player, the examples in this article reveal Helm's strong technique and control. What follows is a sampling of some of his best grooves and licks from the early years of his legendary group, The Band.

Music From Big Pink (1968)
"The Weight"

The Band's first album was born out of sessions with legendary songwriter Bob Dylan (released later as *The Basement Tapes*) that took place in a rented pink house in Woodstock, New York. With a label deal to record their own music, The Band created a landmark ode to Americana. The results sounded like nothing else that was around at the time. Levon Helm, memorably described by producer John Simon as "a bayou folk drummer," conjured up strong imagery both with his voice and with his playing. The drummer's offbeat snare beats and fills add a lilting energy to the slow pace of this classic song. (3:47)

"Chest Fever"

The fill at the end of Garth Hudson's long organ solo in this track is a prime example of Helm's sympathetic rhythmic sense. As Garth uses descending chords to wrap up his solo, Levon's triplets work their way down to his bass drum. This pushes the breaks on the solo section before returning to the intro. (3:34)

"I Shall Be Released"

Levon's delicate snare work highlights the first verse of The Band's take on this famous Bob Dylan song. The rolls in this groove were achieved by Helm turning his snare drum upside down and gently running his fingers across the snare wires. (0:29)

The Band (1969)
"Across The Great Divide"

The self-titled second release from The Band was a high-water mark that solidified the quintet as one of the best ensembles in North America. Continuing in a rootsy vein similar to the first album, *The Band* is filled with timeless songs and wonderful performances. And Levon's quirky drumming is pushed further up front in the mix. The following reoccurring fill from the opening track demonstrates the drummer's ability to incorporate the bass drum into his ideas. (0:53)

"The Night They Drove Old Dixie Down"

Levon's press-roll crescendos in this famous tune set up the chorus hook perfectly, while simultaneously evoking the feel of the Civil War–era subject matter. (0:32)

"When You Awake"

The combination of Helm's offbeat hi-hat pattern over a swung bass drum part gives the chorus of this track an enticing groove. The sound of the snare drum with the snares turned off contributes to the song's "down home" flavor. (0:29)

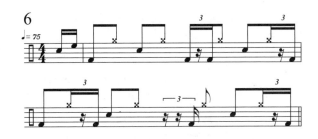

"Up On Cripple Creek"

Here's the intro beat from this classic tune. Rick Danko and Robbie Robertson provide a minimalist bass and guitar riff, leaving Levon's head-bobbing groove to foreshadow what's to come. Notice how Helm avoids the downbeats in most of his bass drum parts, adding to the funkiness of the pattern. (0:00)

TRACK 169

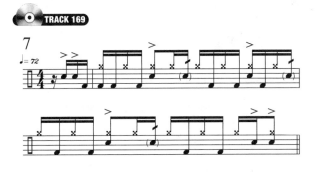

Never one to get locked in to a single pattern, Levon improvises some cool bass and snare combinations in the song's later verses. (2:34)

"Look Out Cleveland"

According to Levon's autobiography, *This Wheel's On Fire*, The Band was making a conscious effort on their second album to employ half-time grooves, which led to different lyric placement and more danceable feels. This track is a prime example. Helm's driving 16th-note ride and syncopated kick pattern are high-energy, while the half-time effect of the snare backbeat delivers a deep pocket. (0:09)

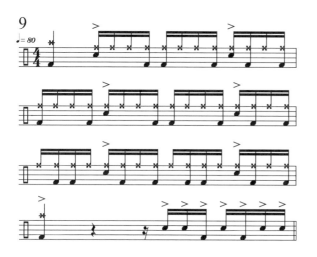

Stage Fright (1970)
"Sleeping"

The third album from The Band moved away from the storytelling imagery of the first two records towards darker, more personal themes dealing with the pressures of success. Todd Rundgren's engineering gave greater clarity to Levon's drum sound, bringing out the subtleties in his cymbal and snare work. A good example is in his jazz-waltz groove for the choruses of this song. (0:59)

TRACK 170

"Stage Fright"

The album's title track features some unique cymbal playing from Helm. Bouncing from straight quarter notes to syncopated 16th-note rhythms, he keeps the song off balance until locking to a straight beat in the choruses. In this intro sequence, notice how the drummer shifts the syncopation from the cymbal to the kick drum. (0:26)

Northern Lights—Southern Cross (1975)
"Acadian Driftwood"

In this beautiful ballad, Levon moves things along with some of his finest ghost-note snare work. It's subtle, but incredibly effective. (1:45)

TRACK 171

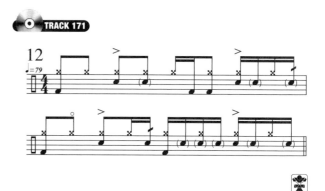

Andrew Lepley

Phillip Halyard

The Drummers Of Steely Dan

MUSIC KEY

open H.H.	O	R.C. Bell •	C.C. ✳
T.T. S.D. F.T. B.D.		
H.H. w/ foot	Rim-Click	Ghost Note

All of Steely Dan's albums are loaded with great drumming. Joining forces in the early '70s as leaders of a quirky rock band, Donald Fagen and Walter Becker gradually evolved the group's sound by increasingly relying on session players for subsequent recordings. By the late '70s, Fagen and Becker had become employers of the finest studio players that New York and Los Angeles had to offer.

All-time drumming giants like Jeff Porcaro, Jim Gordon, Bernard Purdie, Rick Marotta, Steve Gadd, Ed Greene, and Jim Keltner handled the high demands of Steely Dan sessions masterfully, producing some of their finest performances on record. When the band returned to the studio in 2000, a new generation of players, led by drummer Keith Carlock, was called to fill the hot seat. Let's take a look at one classic groove from each Steely Dan album.

Can't Buy A Thrill (1972)
"Do It Again"

Steely Dan's original drummer is often overlooked when compared to the talent the band would later employ. But Jim Hodder was a fine, tasteful player, which is demonstrated on the band's first hit with a simple driving groove that complements Victor Feldman's conga pattern. By not playing the snare on the second beat, Hodder allows the slap of the conga to come through. (0:00)

Countdown To Ecstasy (1973)
"King Of The World"

One of Hodder's best grooves on the second Steely Dan album occurs on the final track. His Latin-tinged hi-hat intro gives way to a funky verse beat that features some excellent left-hand work. (0:23)

Pretzel Logic (1974)
"Pretzel Logic"

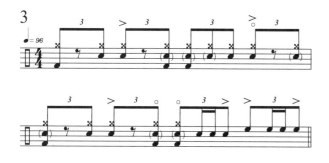

By their third album, Fagen and Becker began to augment the band's lineup with session players, including Jim Gordon and a young Jeff Porcaro on drums. (When the band did a brief tour behind this album, Porcaro and Jim Hodder played together on the tour.) The following two-handed shuffle shows the mature playing of a teenaged Porcaro. (0:16)

Katy Lied (1975)
"Everyone's Gone To The Movies"

Jeff Porcaro is pictured as a bandmember on *Katy Lied* and plays on all but one of the album's tracks. On this tune, he gets to stretch out a little with a cymbal pattern that mirrors the syncopation of the keyboard solo. Notice how Jeff works the bell for effect. The

first measure of this sequence includes a simple drum fill that became a signature for the drummer during this era of his career. (2:06)

The Royal Scam (1976)
"Kid Charlemagne"

Steely Dan's fifth album moved in a decidedly funkier direction, and the groove of legendary R&B drummer Bernard Purdie became an asset. The opening track features Purdie retooling his classic drumbeat from Aretha Franklin's 1971 hit "Rock Steady." The magic of this groove lies in the contrast of the ghost notes against the heavy offbeat accents. (0:48)

Aja (1977)
"Aja"

Steve Gadd's first piece of work for Steely Dan became the signature drum performance of the '70s. In this track, Fagen and Becker gave Gadd not one, but two drum solo spots. Example 6 is the groove Steve settles into after his second solo, as the song moves to a fade-out. Notice his wonderful snare and cymbal work over the samba kick pattern and how he picks up the offbeat accents in the music with his crash cymbal. (7:27)

TRACK 172

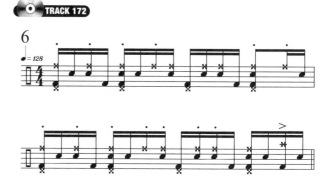

Gaucho (1980)
"Babylon Sisters"

Another of Bernard Purdie's famous grooves (one that he liked to call his "Purdie Shuffle") graces the opening track of the last Steely Dan album from the band's first era. This groove is a textbook example of a rolling triplet shuffle, with the inside notes of the triplets being played as left-hand ghost notes. Other well-known examples of this pattern are Purdie's groove for "Home At Last" on the *Aja* album and Jeff Porcaro's drum track for Toto's "Rosanna." (0:53)

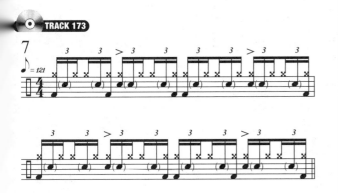

Donald Fagen's The Nightfly (1982)
"Ruby Baby"

On Donald Fagen's first solo album, Jeff Porcaro demonstrated his mastery of the fast triplet groove with the following pattern. Jeff had first turned drummers' heads with a heavier version of this type of pattern on "Hold The Line," a hit from his band Toto's first album in 1978. (0:00)

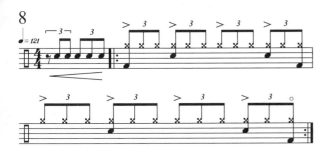

Two Against Nature (2000)
"Negative Girl"

After a twenty-year hiatus, the return of Steely Dan was big news. On this track, studio legend Vinnie Colaiuta finally got his chance to contribute to the band's catalog. And his performance of this reggae groove is breathtaking. Example 9 shows the pattern that he settles into during the guitar solo fade-out. Notice how Vinnie's splashed left-foot hi-hats alternate with the offbeat bell pattern. (4:42)

Everything Must Go (2003)
"Godwhacker"

On this Steely Dan album, Keith Carlock became the first drummer to play on every track since 1973, when Jim Hodder was in the band. One listen to Carlock explains why. His drumming is tasteful and uncluttered, and his groove is impeccable. On this track his ghost notes are so subtle, adding just a touch of ambience to his performance. The range of dynamics between Keith's ghost notes and snare accents is about as extreme as one can get. (0:18)

The Police's
Stewart Copeland
Regatta De Blanc

The worlds of rock and reggae have never been blended more successfully than they were by Sting, Andy Summers, and Stewart Copeland in The Police. After their first album hit with raw punk-type energy, the band settled into reggae-inspired grooves on *Regatta De Blanc*.

Stewart in particular refined his quirky, influential drum style on this 1979 release. All the Copeland-isms are here: the driving quarter-note kick drum with half-time snare, the idiosyncratic hi-hat and rimclick work, the unexpected explosive fills, and a lot more. Let's delve into Copeland's playing on The Police's second album.

"Message In A Bottle"

This section from the album's biggest hit reveals several aspects of Stewart's playing. A classic reggae snare fill leads out of the pounding pre-chorus rock groove. The chorus then moves to a quarter-note kick pattern under a syncopated rimclick flourish. Finally, a nice rimclick/hi-hat tradeoff finishes the sequence. (2:48)

TRACK 176

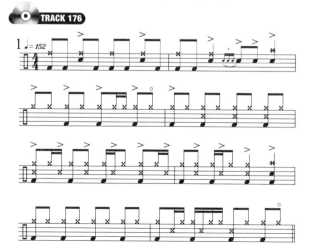

"Bring On The Night"

The chorus beat for this single contains Copeland's two-handed hi-hat rhythms over a 2-and-4 reggae bass drum part. Important details in the groove include the hi-hat triplet, the open hi-hat accents, and the snare crashes. (3:08)

"Deathwish"

Here's another contrasting sequence, showing Stewart's bell work in a fast rock groove, followed by a clave kick pattern with some 16th-note hi-hat embellishments. (3:04)

"Walking On The Moon"

This hit features a half-time reggae shuffle with a broken-up hi-hat pattern and a few extra kick accents. The groove is *deep* on this one. (0:17)

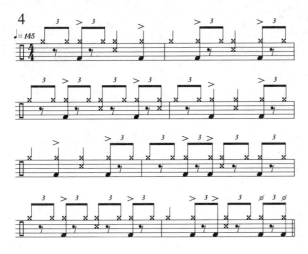

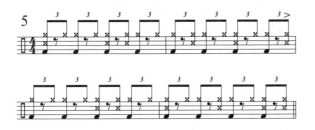

Copeland lifts the chorus of the tune with his quarter-note kick pattern and adlibbed rimclicks. The switch in the bass drum part (from the reggae 2-and-4 to quarter notes) is a reoccurring theme in Stewart's parts on early Police albums. (3:05)

"On Any Other Day"

Stewart composed three songs for this album. This one opens with a favorite lick of his—the fast double flam. The other detail to note is the missing bass drum downbeat, a nod to reggae in a rock pattern. (0:02)

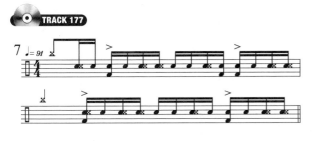

"The Bed's Too Big Without You"

Copeland delivers a great push/pull effect in his beat for this song. His snare and double-time rimclick pattern contrasts with the reggae bass drum part. (1:48)

TRACK 177

"Contact"

The groove from this Copeland composition demonstrates more of his distinctive hi-hat and splash cymbal ideas. (0:25)

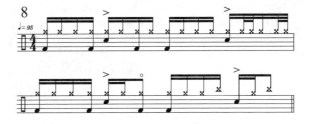

"Does Everyone Stare"

Stewart's final track on the album contains another take on his signature half-time/double-time tradeoff groove. Again, the missing bass drum downbeat plays an important role. (1:05)

"No Time This Time"

The speedy album closer begins with this wild, rolling snare groove. Notice how Copeland retains a bit of the flavor of the intro pattern by adding 16th-notes to the snare part in his verse beat. (0:03)

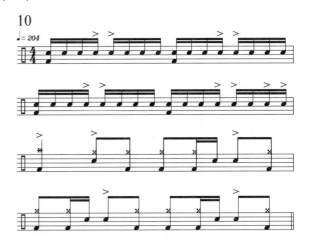

As the song fades out, this blazing fill makes you want to crank up the volume, so you can catch what he just played. (3:07)

The Beatles'
Ringo Starr

#1 Beats

More than thirty years after their breakup, the Beatles phenomenon continues. Their 2000 collection of chart-topping hits, *The Beatles 1*, is one of the biggest-selling albums of all time. New generations raised on rap music and "boy bands" discovered the enduring appeal of the Fab Four. And part of that appeal is the drumming of Ringo Starr.

Ringo's drumming has always been controversial. Technical-minded detractors will point out that he didn't have the "chops" of many modern rock drummers, or couldn't do what contemporaries like Keith Moon and Ginger Baker could do. But Ringo was never one to put himself above the band. His strengths lie in creating the right drum part for the song, a classic approach that proved perfect for the writing of John Lennon, Paul McCartney, and George

Harrison. This explains why the drumming on *The Beatles 1* sounds as fresh today as it did when the band was still together.

Many of Ringo's concepts are widely in use today by players who weren't born when these recordings were made. With unwavering groove, creatively musical ideas, and a marvelous sense of taste, Ringo set the prototype for the modern pop-rock drummer.

Let's go track by track through *The Beatles 1* to examine the essence of Ringo's style. We'll see how he refined his drumming—from the fast-tempo, high-energy early years (tracks 1–10), through his minimalism in the middle period (12–18), to the overdub experiments and loose, rambling feel of the later songs (19–27). Along the way there'll be classic grooves, interesting fills, and a few technically challenging surprises as well.

---

1) "Love Me Do"
The drumming on The Beatles' first single was done by session player Andy White. New to the band at the time, Ringo hadn't yet won producer George Martin's confidence.

2) "From Me To You"
On these early Beatles tracks, listen for Ringo's quirky, energetic fills. This one is from the end of the song's second bridge.

3) "She Loves You"
Here's one of the most famous opening fills and drum grooves of all time. Ringo's charging floor tom rhythm has certainly been used by every rock drummer since.

4) "I Want To Hold Your Hand"

The switch from loose hi-hats to tight into this song's bridge is a great dynamic moment.

Another of Ringo's unusual fills shows up throughout the tune. Not an easy one to pull off at this tempo!

The sound of roaring loose hi-hats was Ringo's signature in the early Beatles years. Here are a couple of examples.

5) "Can't Buy Me Love"

6) "A Hard Day's Night"

7) "I Feel Fine"

For this fast rocker, Ringo chooses a rumba beat, and somehow makes it work.

TRACK 178

8) "Eight Days A Week"

Ringo could swing a shuffle with the best of them. Here he sets up the ending vocal tag.

9) "Ticket To Ride"

Another classic opening fill and groove, this beat is a perfect example of how to be creative and simple at the same time.

10) "Help!"

Ringo slightly swings the 8th notes on Lennon's uptempo rocker. Included is another fast two-handed unison fill.

11) "Yesterday"

No drums.

12) "Day Tripper"

Here's another opening fill showing that Ringo was no slouch on quick single-stroke rolls.

13) "We Can Work It Out"

No fills, no frills. The verse and chorus grooves here are the ultimate in tasteful simplicity.

14) "Paperback Writer"

By this time, Ringo was experimenting with leaving out parts of the traditional drum beat. Here, the stuttering bass and snare pattern (sans hi-hat) perfectly mirrors George Harrison's opening guitar riff.

15) "Yellow Submarine"

More minimalism—no snare drum in the verses of this one. Ringo answers the guitar chords with his bass drum pattern.

16) "Eleanor Rigby"

No drums.

17) "Penny Lane"

Yet another example of Ringo paring back sounds. The hi-hat doubles the snare drum backbeat.

18) "All You Need Is Love"

Here's the ultimate in simplicity—straight quarter notes in the verse. When Ringo switches to the backbeat in the chorus, it lifts the song.

19) "Hello, Goodbye"

After the extended tom fills of "A Day In The Life" (from the *Sgt. Pepper's* album), Ringo began to stretch out more. Here's a four-bar drum break from the first bridge of this tune.

20) "Lady Madonna"

This one contains a double-tracked drum part, which can be clearly heard on the remastered stereo mix of *The Beatles 1*. In the left channel is a classic swing brush pattern in double-time. Ringo overdubs a rock backbeat groove in the right channel. The result is a compelling push/pull feel that drives the song.

21) "Hey Jude"

The famous extended vamp at the end of this song is a great opportunity to study Ringo's unique fills. Here are just two.

22) "Get Back"

Another perfect choice for a groove on a charging tune.

Here's the beat in the bridge and the fill that leads into it.

23) "The Ballad Of John And Yoko"

Paul McCartney played drums on this one. (Ringo was off working on a film at the time.)

24) "Something"

This song's bridge contains another double-tracked drum part: a heavy tom-tom groove overdubbed with a fast triplet tom and hi-hat pattern.

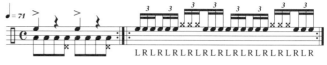

Ringo adds a touch of swing to the end of George's guitar solo.

25) "Come Together"

Yet another all-time famous drum beat. Ringo was a lefty playing a right-handed setup. This may partially explain the unusual sound of many of his fills. Notice how the left-handed sticking in this pattern makes the tom move possible. (See also the triplet overdub in "Something.")

TRACK 179

26) "Let It Be"

Here's Ringo's entrance and groove in the second chorus of this ballad.

And here's an interesting use of toms (another overdub?) in the last verse drum beat.

27) "The Long And Winding Road"

The Beatles *1* closes with a dramatic McCartney ballad. Ringo provides a lighter counterpoint with some deft jazzy cymbal and snare work.

Obviously no one can put a time limit on the popularity of The Beatles. As long as new generations continue to discover these songs, drummers will be influenced by the classic work of Ringo Starr.